Space Cadet!

PD the Pug and the Final Frontier

By PD the Pug

(With help from Mommy Marilee Joyce)

Illustrations by Maria Vyasene

Space Cadet! PD the Pug and the Final Frontier

Printed in the United States of America

Paperback ISBN: 978-1-972446-09-6
Ebook ISBN: 978-1-972446-10-2

INTRODUCTION

Since its opening in 1976, the National Air and Space Museum in Washington, DC, has introduced all things air and space to more than 311 million visitors. The Museum's 60,000 offerings and displays include rockets, jetliners, gliders and other air flight modes as well as everything from space helmets to actually-worn astronaut suits to the teeny-weeny microchips that help make roaming the cosmos possible.

All these amazingly cool treasures are dedicated to human flight and space exploration. And everything at the Air and Space Museum is authentic! The Smithsonian folks say every artifact, every bit of its collection of spacecraft and aircraft and other stuff is real—not some reproduced phony baloney!

These thousands of priceless gems include the Apollo 11 Command Module *Columbia*; the *Friendship 7* capsule, which was flown by that famous guy John Glenn; and the *Spirit of St. Louis*, the single-engine high-wing monoplane that Charles Lindbergh flew solo across the Atlantic in 1927. Not to mention the sound barrier–breaking Bell X-1; the eleven-foot model of the Starship Enterprise that was used to film the original *Star Trek* television show; and the Wright brothers' 1903 Wright Flyer biplane, which is the centerpiece of the museum.

While it is most famous for its collection of what the Air and Space website calls "rare and historically significant" spaceships and spacesuits and other space stuff, the Museum also has thousands of smaller space-related items: engines, medals, trophies, instrumentation, artwork and models. *Plus!* There are films and manuscripts and drawings and documents and oral histories. There are even boots worn on the moon that are still covered in lunar dust. A lot of space in that big space!

But the object collection includes fascinating artifacts of terrestrial flight, too. We're talking amazing stuff like a letter from George Washington about American ballooning; an unbroken teacup and saucer recovered from the wreckage of the Hindenburg; and a doggie sweater that was worn by aerobatic pilot Art Scholl's dog, Aileron! So much stuff! So many cool air and space gadgets and gewgaws and golly-look-at-that goodies!

But, as swell as all those items are, soon no one will be talking about them.

That's because we are about to see the unveiling of exhibit number 60,001—the Air and Space Museum's most prestigious, most treasured, most significant artifact yet! A piece of paraphernalia representing none other than Spacedog PD the Pug!

Yep, by the time you read this, PD the Astrodog will have returned from his mission to space. Me! The National Aeronautics and Space Administration's newest and best space spelunker, cosmos cowboy, galaxy gadabout. *Me!* Out there in outer space!

Okay, okay, so I don't exactly have an aerospace degree; I didn't go to some Astrodog University of anything. But no matter! Mommy always calls me the flightiest dog in the universe, and apparently NASA agrees!

It all started when Mommy saw an announcement about NASA's search for an American dog to be the first canine ever to accompany the crew of a US space mission. Tens of thousands of dogs entered the contest for the privilege of going on the farthest-ever walkie. Er, flightie. But the heavens were on my side: NASA chose *me*! And now I am about to actually head off into those very heavens.

Between 1951 and 1966, forty-eight Soviet and two Chinese dogs were sent into space. Yet no canine from the United States has ever ventured into that final frontier. We have sent monkeys, chimpanzees, mice, rats, spiders, bullfrogs, brine shrimp, sea urchins, bobtail squid, tardigrades—even insects such as fruit flies. But never a dog. Certainly never a pug.

That's about to change. Your pal PD will soon be the first-ever dog from the United States to go into orbit.

It is estimated that more than 600 million people tuned in to watch the Apollo 11 moon landing in 1969. Well, big whoop! When PD the PugNaut and crew launch into orbit next month, every television, radio, podcast, blogcast, dog-cast—all the casts!—will be focused on Me, Me, Me! The soon-to-be most famous space traveler of all time.

Hold my (nonalcoholic dog) beer, Michael Jackson fans. I'm about to show the world how moonwalking is done!

NASA
Dognaut
Application

Chapter One

WHERE NO PUG HAS GONE BEFORE

Readers of my second book, *No, YOU Sit! PD the Pug's Manual for How to Train Your Human,* know that I'm not a fan of costumes. Mommy has bought me so many dog outfits over the years that she actually created a PD clothing closet in our garage. Should you wish to get a chuckle at my expense, you can take a video tour of the clothes closet (@pdthepug on Instagram, March 28, 2023) as well as see hundreds of posts of me posing.

God already gave me a super cute outfit. It's called *fur.* We dogs are dressed and ready to go from womb to tomb. The only time I want fabric on my frame is when it's freezing or raining, which . . . wait, why am I outside when it's freezing or raining?

Well, there is one outfit I'm happy to wear anytime: my space-dog togs! Lord, do I look splashy, sporty, spiffy and splendid when I'm decked out as PD the Pug, America's first dognaut! As I proudly pose for the gathered media alongside the crew of the *Wolf Wanderer* spacecraft that very shortly will blast off into space, my mind is all swirly and whirly over everything that's happened in such a short amount of time. I am still chasing my tail in excitement over being chosen—although only in my thoughts right now, since Mommy said a small black whirlwind might cause a distraction at the launch day press conference.

Six months or so ago, the National Aeronautics and Space Administration announced a nationwide search for America's first spacedog. One hundred finalists would undergo "fun and challenging" tests regarding "food, fitness and focus," and the winner would accompany four human astronauts into orbit. More than just being a furry friend to the flight crew, the winning canine would participate in all sorts of scientific experiments and research while in orbit. The entry form was a bit vague on the details, but it assured entrants that the selected fur baby would contribute tons to NASA, America and the whole world.

NASA partnered with national and local dog retailers to spread the word about the cosmic contest. Mommy spotted the display table advertising the contest when she went to PetSmart to replace my bed that *someone* basically destroyed the night prior whilst having a nightmare about my sworn enemy Ralph the Dog (see all prior PD the Pug books) taking a walkie with my Fawn Girl Pug Crush and marking over my weewee while she watched.

"PD! PD, come here, my little astrodog!" she'd shouted out gleefully as she'd raced through the front door with a bagged bed balanced in her arms, hustling to drop it on the floor where my old one used to lie. Ignoring what I was hoping was my most persuasive "dinner is five minutes late" guilt-trip squint, she'd swooped down and scooped stunned little me into her arms and laughed as she waltzed us around the kitchen.

Thankfully, before my twirl-enhanced, now-ten-minutes-past-dinnertime dizziness could pull me under, Mommy stopped dancing and carried me to the counter, set me down, and then reached into her purse for the NASA entry form. "This, PD, *this*," she said, waving it in front of my googly eyes, "is for a contest seeking a dog to go into space!"

As she read me the words from NASA—words aimed at making American dog parents believe their precious pooch could reach for the literal stars—I momentarily forgot dinner and started imagining *me*, PD the Pug, as PD the PugNaut. I could already feel the insulation of my puffy spacesuit, its rigidity and bulk surrounding me with a pressurized environment; I could feel the helmet around my round head, its strong plastic keeping me safe, its design helping me breathe; I could feel my little backpack with my oxygen tank secured to my sturdy back; I could feel the small thruster jets on the back of my suit, there to help if I (gulp) somehow floated away from my spaceship . . .

I'm PD the PugNaut! I'm PD the PugNaut! I'm PD the PugNaut! I'm . . .

"PD, don't jump!" Mommy cried out as she lunged toward the counter to grab me mid leap. So entranced and engrossed was I in my *Guardian PD of the Galaxy* fantasy that I had closed my eyes and imagined the countertop was my own launch pad into the Final Frontier. Good thing Commander Mommy had aborted the mission before I blasted off.

Well! Fast-forward six months, and I *am* about to blast off!

Mommy and thousands of other American doggie parents had filled out the form and then headed to mailboxes and post offices, stars in their eyes as they imagined their fur babies up in the sky among *actual* stars. Dogs representing countless breeds in every canine class were entered into the big competition for the honor of being the first American dog to go into orbit.

Candidates were screened for good health (check!), good temperament and ability to be cooperative with a human crew (no problem!), and "trainability" so as to be receptive to learning and obeying both common and new commands (fake it 'til you make it, PD!).

Screening narrowed the massive pool of entrants to just one hundred dogs, including yours truly. Then the battle began. The several tests we underwent included a zero-G fetch test (that basset hound tripped over his own ears!); space food tasting (good: dehydrated bacon chews; bad: freeze-dried liver lumps); refraining from howling in a helmet (the baying beagle and chatty chihuahua were sunk!); and learning to poopie on the vacuum-suction toilet (I thought that skinny greyhound was going to be sucked into the void!).

Based on those tests, ten finalists were selected. Me and the nine other dogs then competed in one last challenge. And neither Mommy nor I could believe our luck that a challenge so easy peasy for me would determine the winner!

Readers of my previous books will recall that I am an award-winning zoomer and tail chaser. So imagine my glee when the ten of us were led to a centrifuge machine, which simulates the high G-forces that astronauts experience during launch and reentry. Basically a tail-chasing zoomie machine on steroids! While the about-to-be runners-up were stumbling dizzily about and vomiting up that morning's kibble, yours truly was merely lightheaded with joy, hoping and praying the judges saw that I had spun circles around the competition.

A week later—a week with several time-outs in my crate for nearly digging an anxiety-fueled hole in Mommy's white living-room rug—we reached the big day. Mommy and every other dog mommy and daddy gathered around their TVs, radios, laptops, tablets and phones as the winner was revealed. I can still hear the NASA man's deep voice, still see Mommy's stunned face, still feel the never-before-equaled excitement deep in my little pug bones.

"This is the National Aeronautics and Space Administration with an important announcement! After poring over thousands of applications from wonderful and worthy American dogs, we have chosen the first-ever American dognaut. This dog will have the honor of accompanying our flight crew on the spaceship *Wolf Wanderer* . . ."

By this point, Mommy had picked me up and was squeezing me so tightly against her that I thought I'd pass out as the

NASA man dramatically paused and stared into the camera—and, I swear, directly into my own big round eyes—and boomed:

"Big congratulations to Mr. PD the Pug of Arlington, Virginia! I am sure PD and his Mommy join me in recognizing the courage and hope of those dogs not selected as PD humbly accepts this great honor, and . . ."

And while PD beat out all the other applicants, it's especially notable that he once again defeated that slimy slimeface slimeball Ralph the Dog, who wouldn't be able to find outer space with the Hubble Telescope and a Google Space map, and who will be home in his doghouse while PD the PugNaut is up in the heavens doing lots of groundbreakingly crucial experiments that will change the whole world for the better, and . . .

"PD? PD, wake up!" I startled awake to find Mommy fanning me with the *Space Exploration for Dummies* book she had bought to learn some good buzzwords and phrases for the essay part of the application that helped lead to my big win. "I think you fainted, sweetie."

Well of *course* I fainted. Because basically I had just become NASA's mascot! And I could only fantasize about what that might mean. Parades? Statues? Proclamations? Lifetime Chewy discounts? Who's to say . . .

So, back to the very out-of-this-world present: It's blastoff day! Your favorite spacedog PD and the other four members of the *Wolf Wanderer* crew are proudly standing on a media platform outside the John F. Kennedy Space Center, the primary launch center for big stars like yours truly who are heading off to do important research and conduct important experiments among the real stars in outer space. I can only imagine how huge of a paw print my little pug paw is going to leave on science. I probably will win the PD the Pug Puglitzer for Cosmic Contribution.

But that comes later! Right now, I am on the portable stage alongside my crewmates, facing dozens of media from around the world who are gathered here at Cape Canaveral for this momentous moment. Like the rest of my team, I am sporting a shirt featuring a noble wolf, our canine ancestor who—clearly *exactly* like me—was built for strength and endurance. NASA officials told the press that *Wolf Wanderer* beat out other mission names because, like NASA itself, the wolf is devoted to its pack, strategically calculating, and relentless in pursuit of its goals.

Obviously, like me. Obviously, nothing like Ralph. Who lost.

I am showing a supersized snaggletooth smile to each print and television reporter yelling my name—"Over here, PD!" . . . "PD! Give me a grin for *Dog Day* Magazine!" . . . "PD! How about a little tail wag for our cameraman?"—while my four crewmates do likewise for the media throng gathered for this historic happening. I haven't felt this chuffed, this cheerful, this chipper since that time I was hiding behind a tree and espied my Fawn Girl Pug Crush enjoying a whiff of my weewee on a bush.

"Psst, PD! PD!!"

I quiet Madonna's *Vogue! Vogue! Vogue!*–chanting voice in my head and spot Mommy at the front of the roped-off VIP section to the left of the gathered press. She's waving her arms around like some crazed fan trying to get the attention of *America's! First! Dognaut!*, and the flash after flash from her iPhone's camera is earning her some serious stink eye from the gathered paparazzi, who want my snagglesmile focused on them and not on the deranged woman in the *Beam Me Up, PD!* T-shirt.

For the first half hour or so, I smile and wave from my seat at a long table as the NASA public relations team answer questions about my selection and about the backgrounds of my crewmates. Then suddenly an important-looking man in a dark suit with the NASA insignia enamel pin on his lapel appears and takes his place behind a podium. America's spacedog PD and the rest of the *Wolf Wanderer* crew rise as the man reaches into his breast pocket, pulls out a small stack of note cards, and places them on the podium's slanted top before beaming a wide grin at the audience.

"Ladies and gentlemen," the man begins. He scans the crowd, chuckling as he takes in Mommy's tee, then takes a deep breath and squares his shoulders. "I am NASA Administrator George Jetson the Third, and I am here to welcome you to what we at NASA consider to be among the most notable, most incredible, most astounding, most electrifying moments in this agency's history.

"Not since the *Eagle* landed and Neil Armstrong descended its ladder to become the first human being to walk on the moon have I and my colleagues been this moved and delighted by what can only be called yet another giant leap forward for NASA and, by extension, for mankind.

"Because while the United States has outperformed other nations in countless ways—in the space race; in the effort to explore the solar system; and in the contributions our researchers have made to science, medicine, transportation, education, the environment, industry and more—there is one metric by which we have lagged lamentably. Until now."

The crowd murmurs in anticipation, some leaning into one another and whispering excitedly, many raising phones to snap pictures of whatever is coming next as Administrator Jetson pauses. Then—his trembling lips betraying the strong emotion he is trying to suppress—he turns to face the *Wolf Wanderer* crew, nodding at each member of our little team in turn until he reaches my snagglesmiley, stoked but slightly shaky self.

"PD the Pug, with whom I am proud to share this stage, will soon be NASA's first-ever—*America's* first-ever—canine astronaut to go into orbit!" Administrator Jetson pauses to salute—actually *salute!*—me while Mommy leaps to her feet, causing the rest of the audience to rise en masse and applaud.

When the applause finally ends, Administrator Jetson brings out a small box from behind the podium and then grins widely as he reaches in to retrieve what's inside. I sure hope it's kibble; I'm famished from all this exciting hustle-bustle. But as he pulls it out, I sigh. Alas, no food—but a "treat" for me nonetheless.

"PD, engineers at NASA have created—just for you, just for this monumental mission—a special *Wolf Wanderer* collar." He pauses to hold it out so that my crewmates and

I can see this invention that has caused the delighted look on his face. From where I stand, I can make out the embroidered brave-looking wolves that will encircle my little pug neck. I feel strong and intimidating, and I'm not even wearing it yet!

"PD, if your Mommy would kindly join us on the stage, we will swap out your collar for this sleek, stylish new one, which, as everyone can see, features the mission logo: the confident, resourceful, self-assured, hungry—in our case, hungry for scientific answers—wolf! But this collar is more than a fashion item or souvenir. PD, this ultramodern, innovative, futuristic, dare I say 'space-age' collar contains microelectronics that will allow Mission Control to better monitor your actions and reactions while you undergo lots of fun research and experiments in space! And"—here Administrator Jetson tee-hees and wags his finger at me—"it will let us know where you are at all times, so that you can't get yourself into any trouble during the mission!"

What?? I huff inwardly, trying my best to continue beaming my full snagglegrin and not betray the bother that is bouncing around my cerebrum. *If I'd known that I, Earth's most famous PugNaut, would have to wear an ankle bracelet around my neck, I might have rethought this gig!*

I'm snapped out of my little snit by a whirlwind of activity in the front row of the audience. Mommy has leapt from her seat and is giving those nearest her a proud pirouette before dancing her way up the steps to the platform. I hope I am masking my mortification as my crewmates and

Administrator Jetson give her a round of polite applause and the latter reaches out his hand to help her up onto the stage.

“Welcome, PD’s Mommy!” Mr. Jetson exclaims, his eyes twinkling as he seats her next to me behind the long table. He holds aloft this smiley-wolf-decorated *spy! snoop! spook! meddling mole!* collar as he looks from her to me and back again. “PD’s Mommy, I can’t begin to imagine your pride as you witness PD accompanying the *Wolf Wanderer* mission team into the heavens, where he will help conduct research and undergo tests that no doubt will lead to leaps in our nation’s educational, technological, corporate and scientific sectors.”

As the administrator pauses to glance at his notes, it’s all I can do to contain the zoomie monster fighting to possess me. True, I’m not keen on the collar that’s about to monitor my every move, but I sure am keen on *me!* I zone out, imagining PD the PugNaut pinwheeling around the podium and out into the audience. *A blur of fur! A blaze of blackness! Scurrying and hurrying! Whizzing and whipping and whisking and whirling and . . .*

“Psst! PD! Pay attention, sweetie!”

I snap to, getting a grip on my inner gyrations as Mommy’s pink-nail-polish-manicured hands reach to remove my usual collar.

Administrator Jetson, standing tall over her shoulder, passes her my new neckwear. As she clicks it in place, I catch my reflection in Mommy’s sunglasses and think I look pretty swanky in my new *Mata Hari meddling!* collar. I stare for a moment at the expression on the wolf logo’s face, imagining becoming one with my canine ancestors, all their strength and courage and resourcefulness becoming mine . . .

PD the PugNaut: On the prowl for NASA progress! Hunting the heavens! Voraciously validating and verifying the variables of our . . .

"PD—heh-heh!—easy there, my little wolfnaut," Administrator Jetson titters as I return to Earth from the orbit of my daydream, which apparently had me skulking to and fro across the stage à la PD the Wolf: tail tucked, ears back, head down, sniffing and whiffing as I hunted for thermostabilized, irradiated space food or something.

As I shed my adopted wolf persona and return to my seat at the end of the crew table, the administrator continues:

"Ladies and gentlemen of the press and our gathered friends, I know you all must feel as I do: like you have a front row seat to history as NASA's 'pawsome' pug PD and the other esteemed members of the *Wolf Wanderer* crew prepare for launch. Five hours from now, they will be in orbit, where they will work to further NASA's contributions to our country and world, one experiment at a time."

I look over at the four humans with whom I'll be sharing a space in space for the next several days, their big smiles and puffed chests making clear the excitement and pride they each feel about the mission on which we momentarily will embark. I look out into the audience and see Mommy reseated in the front row, looking nearly as delighted as the day she brought baby PD home from Howling Hills Kennel. I look at Administrator Jetson, who has retaken his spot at the podium, from where he is giving huge grins to me and the rest of the spaceflight team. And I look up, into the sky, the gigantic and expansive sky . . . boundless, vast, infinite and incomprehensible. And I squint my googlies as squinty as a pug can and try my hardest to look beyond the blue, imagining the other planets and asteroids and meteors and the billions upon billions of stars all around us.

And in my mind's eye, I see me, PD the PugNaut, the biggest star of them all. Bigger than Betelgeuse. As big as red supergiant Stephenson 2-18, the biggest star in the known universe, its radius two thousand times that of Earth's sun! Bigger than *that,* even! And as Administrator Jetson ushers us five *Wolf Wanderer* wanderers off the platform and toward the spacecraft, I think: *You got this, PD.*

Gulp . . .

CAPE CANAVERAL
MISSION ANNOUNCEMENT
NASA
NASA
WW
MISSION
NASA
WW
MISSION
NASA
WW
MISSION
NASA
Beam Me
Up, PD

NASA
NASA
MISSION

Chapter Two

HOUSTON, WE HAVE A PD PROBLEM

> "*Houston to* Wolf Wanderer, *Houston to* Wolf Wanderer . . ."
>
> *"Go ahead, Houston."*
>
> "Wolf Wanderer, *we are detecting nocturnal activity near the kibble storage bins. PD's collar camera is broadcasting what appears to be several dozen small brown circular foodstuffs floating around in the galley. Please advise."*
>
> *"Roger that, Houston. Please stand by . . ."*

Stupid spy collar! I can't believe it already ratted me out!

It's the first day of the mission, the first day that I am representing the USA as the country's first dog in space. A dog whose role is to make the nation proud as I participate in research that leads to all kinds of innovations and creations and developments and advancements back home. A dog who is expected to exemplify a certain level of dignity and decorum. A dog whom other dogs idolize and follow as they decide how to compose and conduct their comparatively less notable, less exceptional lives.

So this is not a great start: we lifted off from Cape Canaveral just five hours ago, and I'm already sensing an impending time-out in my crate—or wherever you get a time-out in a spaceship. A time-out that sure is not deserved! As I am sure you'll agree after reading my side!

Look, all I wanted was a morsel or two of sustenance after what was among both the most exciting and most exhausting days of my seven-years-long life. After the press conference ended and the crowd left, Mommy accompanied me and the crew as some super big-shot-looking NASA people escorted us onto a fancy bus for the ride to the launchpad. As we got closer, Mommy pointed out the gleaming white spaceship emblazoned with the mission's magnificent wolf mascot and the round blue NASA logo.

When we finally reached the launchpad, one of my crewmates held out his arms to take me with them. Mommy squeezed me so tight I thought the NASA heavies would have to pry me from her arms, but, with a final kiss on my round pug head, she handed me over and waved a teary, cheery farewell.

We spent our first few minutes in orbit getting accustomed to zero gravity. My crewmates pushed off with their feet and did a sort of arm-swimming thing. Mine was more like a doggy paddle. So fun! Then we explored what will be our digs for the next several days. *Wolf Wanderer* has a combo laboratory and workspace; a galley, smaller than Mommy's kitchen; a pantry (clearly this is my new happy place!); a storage area; an air lock chamber for entering and exiting the spacecraft; a medical bay for booboos; a potty area; an entertainment room for break times; and a small gym with treadmills, bikes and some dumbbells, which is what these humans *are* if they think I am going to be exercising beyond this fun zero-G-flying-around thing.

Our tour complete, I spent the next several minutes checking out my crewmates. There's a tall, lanky man with black hair who laughs a lot; a small woman with yellow hair and cat-eye glasses who waves her hands around when she talks; a man with no hair who seems nerdy to me because he keeps using words like *cryogenic* and *syzygy* and *Oumuamua*; and a red-haired man who always seems to be studying big thick books and also seems obsessed with checking and rechecking buttons and switches . . . which is worrying me, because didn't the NASA nabobs already check everything?

Wearied from ninety minutes of touring and sizing up my mates and then two hours of going over the research tasks assigned to us, I feigned needing to practice my floating skills and air-swam away from the gang and over to the galley to sneak a snack or two. Since I hadn't had a chance to really investigate the food situation during our initial walkie through the rocket, I was excited to have a proper prying into the pantry.

Wow! I will have to suggest a pantry layout like this to Mommy. There are all these cubbies and cabinets and bins, each labeled with its contents. DEHYDRATED PROTEIN . . .

FREEZE-DRIED FRUIT . . . REHYDRATABLE VEGETABLES . . . POWDERED CONDIMENTS . . . dozens of different foods that just need a bit of reconstituting before chow time.

My googlies goggled at the galactic goodies, then suddenly landed on what any *compos mentis* canine would consider the *crème de la crème*: Kibble!

Globules of floating pug drool slowly circled my head as I read the labels on a row of bins at the far end of the pantry. KIBBLE BIN ONE . . . KIBBLE BIN TWO . . . KIBBLE BIN THREE . . . KIBBLE BIN FOUR . . . KIBBLE BIN FIVE. Five! *Five* great big bins full of kibble! And humans don't like kibble (I never see Mommy getting into my food the way I try and get into hers), and so I realized *all this kibble is for me!* Are we high up enough for this to be considered *Heaven*?

Delirious with desire, I paddled my furry forelimbs through the airspace between me and Kibble Bin One and said a quick prayer that opposing thumbs are not a requisite for opening the *Wolf Wanderer* food containers. As I pressed my flat face against a button on the lid of the bin, I had to mentally muzzle myself from doing a happy howl.

Wait! What's happening? Nooooo! I had forgotten all about that "no gravity" thing. As soon as the container opened, fully one-fourth of the PD fare rose out in slow motion and began drifting all around the pantry. Posthaste, I paddled my paws and nuzzled the lid shut. But it was too late; there were what had to be hundreds of pieces of kibble floating around me. In any other setting this would have been among the happiest sights imaginable. But not here. Not now. Not mere meters away from a group of astronauts expecting a PugNaut with his Ps and Qs prioritized.

What a disaster! The voice of the NASA administrator booming over the comm system meant my snooping, snitching collar had alerted him and my crewmates to my sneaking around snatching snacks!

So here I am in full PD freak-out mode, and all because—per usual—I prioritized my belly over my better self, who would not have freed the dog food and would already be back in the lab studying tasks and getting better acquainted with my team. Now I am caroming, bouncing, ricocheting like a pinball, smashing and bashing, thudding and thunking and thumping into any and every surface as my wide pug maw gulps in all the goodies I can reach.

Mommy always admonishes me for eating too fast; Lord, if she could see me now. I have never sucked in more succulence so swiftly. I swallow the final yummy kibble and repress a big belch just before the pantry door flies open and the researcher astronaut and his smiley sidekick float in.

"Houston," says the smiley one with a happy lilt in his announcement, "we have PD. Repeat: We have PD."

"Roger. What is he up to? Over."

The researcher one studies me studiously, squinting a bit as he looks from me to the food bins and back again.

"Houston," he reports, "it seems PD was just touring around, getting a feel for the spacecraft and its amenities. Clearly a good use of his time following his earlier diligent study of the mission assignments with us in the lab. We don't see any foodstuffs. Maybe his collar camera was facing a viewport and showed stars or something."

"Roger. Houston out."

Phew. That was a close call, I think as I watch my two crewmates air-swim away from Kibble Bin One. I will have to figure out a way to disable this undercover collar. Or turn the camera around so it's buried in my fur. I can't sneak food from Eden, er, Kibble Bin Row, with this high-tech noose narcing me out to Administrator Jetson every time I move a muscle.

But for now I'm in the clear and need to do what I said was important: get to know my teammates. I reenter the research room, where the four humans are huddled around a whiteboard poring over the tasks listed on it and brainstorming the best ways to tackle each test.

"Oh, look who's back! Come join us, Mr. PugNaut!" calls out the blonde woman as she unbelts herself from her seat and practically springs over to me. "We were just discussing the correct length and strength for your paw springs and bungee cord."

Paw springs? Bungee cord?

Looking past my nonplussed noggin to address the egghead part of the quartet, blondie holds her whiteboard marker aloft and waves it around like she's writing in the air or something. "I know there are things I'm forgetting; what else does PD need for his role in our experiments?"

"Roger, there sure are," asserts the researcher man while wagging his forefinger in a professorial manner. "I've gone over the test procedures multiple times and see that PD will require an enhanced odor-detecting mask, goggles, a moisture-wicking track suit and of course his dognaut spacesuit in the event of an EVA."

"Oh, of course! Roger!"

The egghead one butts in. "Roger, but before you secure the perineal access port, be sure to check the placement of the superabsorbent polymer composite to facilitate efficient sequestration of bodily fluid and fecal matter."

"Roger!" the smiley one laughs. "Wouldn't want PD turds floating about!"

"Roger!" the other three yell in unison as they high-five one another, guffawing at my expense.

I'm about to ask who and where this lady Eva is when a baffling thought beams into my brain. *Everyone here is named Roger. Even the woman astronaut. Why do they all have the same name? Do humans have to be named Roger to be considered for space school? Are they going to rename* me*?*

Looking from one Roger to the next, I decide I am more curious about my spacesuit and these other gewgaws and gizmos and gadgets than about what's in a name. My googlies are drawn to researcher Roger, who is flipping through a book titled *Conversion Tables: Canine Clothing and Accessory Measurements Based on Thoracic Dimensions and Head Shape*

I paw-stroke my way over to get a closer look at the book. I paddle in place as hard as my little pug legs allow to keep from drifting all over the joint, and I focus on following researcher Roger's pointer finger as it runs across a section headed "Pug Paw Proportions: Measuring Forepaw vs. Hindfoot."

Ah, this must be for my mysterious "paw springs." I am both excited and frightened as I contemplate those and the other items. Why do my paws need to be outfitted with springs? Why do I need a bungee cord? And what on Earth—er, what in Space is a "perineal access port"?

And who is Eva?!?

"Hmm, this is curious," egghead Roger says, looking over his colleague's shoulder at the Pug Paw Proportions page. "Says here that the canine manus, or forelimb, and the pes, or hindlimb, have several parts. For example, the digital pad—often called the toe bean—is composed of keratinized skin and provides shock absorption and . . ."

"Yes, yes, Roger! We needn't get a lecture on PD's latest pedicure," laughs smiley Roger. "Let's just measure his paws already!"

The now-deflated egghead Roger sulkily pats the airspace between us and reaches for a fancypants measuring doodad bearing the NASA logo. I drift closer and warily extend my left forepaw toward him just as researcher Roger raises his hand and clears his throat.

"I was just rechecking our assignment, and it says PD will need to spring two meters during the squirrel chasing sequence. So I think it's necessary to doublecheck the dimensions of his dewclaws and carpal pads, because . . ."

As the Rogers drone on about my feet, which I heretofore considered important only insofar as they aid my strutting from one bush to the next to mark over Ralph the Dog's weewee, I have totally tuned out my teammates and now am focused solely on one thought:

There's going to be a squirrel chasing?? Get those springs on me already!

All four Rogers now circle 'round me with notepads and measuring tapes and protractors and vernier calipers and other doodads and doohickeys to precisely procure all PD proportions. A couple hours later, I have been measured and weighed to fine-tune the fit of all the accoutrements I will need for PD R&D. And I am absolutely beat! Lord, do I need some nourishment. Who knew it could be so wearying to just hold my barrel-bodied self stock-still in midair?

After the Rogers finish with me and then review their task lists to ensure maximum ergonomic efficiency, researcher Roger stares at a rectangular device about the size of Mommy's microwave oven and then at his wristwatch and back again.

"I was just checking the Atomic Deep Space Clock," he says. "We are now seventeen minutes past the time I scheduled for dinner."

"Oh, don't be so punctilious," snaps egghead Roger. "Our evening repast consists of rehydrating desiccated food, not savoring haute cuisine."

I tune the Rogers out again as smiley Roger giggles and Rogerette grabs the whiteboard from the air next to her and attaches it to the wall with Velcro to prevent it from drifting about while we sup. As the gang motion for me to follow them to the dining area, I find myself in a headspace quite unfamiliar to me:

We aren't going to get the squirrel now? We're going to eat now?

Apologizing to any pug spirits in space who might have sensed my ranking squirrel-chasing over belly-filling, I paddle my paws to the galley, where smiley Roger is microwaving a pouch labeled CHICKEN AND VEGETABLES. Other pouches, cans and foil packages in the pile for tonight read BEEF STEAK AND MASHED POTATOES, PIZZA, SHRIMP COCKTAIL, BUTTERSCOTCH PUDDING and APPLESAUCE. I also spy several vacuum-sealed powdered drink pouches and a bunch of powdered condiment packets.

My drool floats up and circles my round head. Alas. Knowing that—unlike at home with easy-to-guilt-trip Mommy—these humans aren't about to share any of their rehydrated yummies, I air-swim over to Kibble Bin One. I feign patience as I hope that the Rogers notice the hungry-looking PugNaut who hath not. Amazingly, it is my adversary the spy collar that comes to my rescue, saving me from impending deprivation and want.

"Houston to *Wolf Wanderer*, Houston to *Wolf Wanderer*," comes the now-familiar voice of Administrator Jetson.

"Go ahead, Houston," responds egghead Roger as he reaches for plates and utensils.

"Roger, *Wolf Wanderer*. PD's collar is showing PD at the kibble storage area again," the NASA chief says. "We are just checking to see whether this is another possible collar camera malfunction or if PD is getting into his food without assistance."

Smiley Roger cackles as he spots me sitting on my rump in front of the kibble container. "No problemo, Houston. Looks like our little astropug is flying a bit light in the belly. In fact, he looks as ravenous as the wolves circling his neck!"

Researcher Roger looks at the bin, then at me. Then he does some counting on his fingers and turns to the other Rogers.

"As we ascertained during our weighing and measurement groundwork, PD weighs 14.6 pounds. By my estimation, PD should receive 27 to 30 pieces of kibble per meal. This, of course, will be impacted by the size of each piece as well as the amount of physical activity he has engaged in that day. Also, there is the matter of when he most recently passed urine or defecated, because . . ."

"For goodness' sake!" Rogerette interjects, silencing her crewmate as she quickly unlatches Kibble Bin One—careful to open only the small hole that fits the attached tongs instead of flipping up the whole lid like *someone* did during his pantry probe. She reaches for my special zero-G dog dish with its slit that allows me to suck out one morsel at a time—which thankfully will prevent a repeat of the flying food incident—and begins to unhook the tongs.

"Whoa. Hold up, please," intones egghead Roger, causing a suspension of Operation Feed PD. My snagglesmile turns into a fangy frown as I watch him float over to Kibble Bin One with a confused expression on his face. He then peers into the bin, taps his forehead like an erudite professor, and sticks some sort of measuring instrument into its contents.

"Our internal resource allocation system is indicating missing food units." Egghead Roger's eyes travel from one Roger to the next and then land on my innocence-feigning face. "It seems a superabundance of PD's comestibles has taken a quantum leap into another dimension, because . . ."

"Hey! Hold on there!" researcher Roger says indignantly. "I checked every bin on *Wolf Wanderer* prior to takeoff, and you can be certain all containers had the amounts allocated by NASA and are in strict accordance with all regulations!"

"Roger that," says egghead Roger. "But then, please explain to me why Kibble Bin One has undergone a significant biomass reduction!"

As researcher Roger and egghead Roger continue quarreling over kibble quantity, and as Rogerette and smiley Roger alternate between playing catch with and teasing me with the tongs that I wish someone were using right now to fill my bowl, a scary thought breaks through my glucose-craving brain:

The Rogers are going to tell Administrator Jetson to recheck the videotape! And he'll see that I stole all that kibble! Diversion needed! Diversion needed! There has to be a way to get the Rogers away from Kibble Bin One! I can't let them do a comprehensive kibble count!

Ah! I might know one way to vacate the area . . .

"Lord Almighty!" shrieks Rogerette as she lets go of the tongs-*cum*-fetching-stick and frantically waves her hand in front of her confused face. "What on Earth is that stench?"

"I don't know!" shouts the normally smiley Roger, for once appearing to find no mirth in the moment. "Did someone rehydrate a past-its-prime hard-boiled egg?"

"Well, it certainly does mimic the scent of sulfur compounds, perhaps as a result of bacterial fermentation," egghead Roger says. "However, this malodorous fetidness smells distinctly like . . . like . . . like . . ."

As one, at once, all the Rogers swivel around and glare at me. In unison they yell:

"PD, did you *fart*?"

Pasting a pretend look of apology on my face, I cast my eyes downward in faux shame as the Rogers hurriedly arm-paddle out of the pantry. The moment the fourth member of the Roger quartet is out of eyesight, I make my move. I hurry-scurry to Kibble Bin One and, for the second time on my first day in space, pop open its latch, sending all its kibble floating into the kitchen and beyond. *Ha! No way to weigh now!* I'm feeling like the universe's most smug pug until . . .

"Houston to *Wolf Wanderer,* Houston to *Wolf Wanderer,*" the voice of Administrator Jetson booms through the comm system, ending any hope of my getting away with either this bin break-in or the one I committed earlier.

Rogerette bounces in, the fingers of her left hand plugging her nose as her left hand presses her headset to her ear. She releases her nose, bats away the dozens of kibble bits circling her blonde head, and then slowly, warily takes a breath, testing the air before responding.

"Go ahead, Houston."

"Roger. *Wolf Wanderer,* PD's collar again is transmitting imagery suggestive of airborne brown food bits. My apologies if this is another false alarm, but given that the particles match those seen in the earlier video feed, we would be remiss to not check in."

I'm sunk! I fret and fuss inwardly as fear displaces hunger in priority ranking. *Completely sunk! How am supposed to make NASA glad I won the Dognaut contest if I start off in the Dognaut House?*

Shaking her head at me, Rogerette replies to the boss. "Houston, we regret to report there is no error on your end. We wish there were, but no. PD apparently opened Kibble Bin One, sending all its contents airborne. We now believe he additionally caused the earlier—"

"Roger!" Administrator Jetson interrupts, adding a bit of admonishment to his tone as the rest of the Rogers reenter the kitchen and gather 'round the speakers. "But, *Wolf*

Wanderer, our Deep Space Atomic Clock shows PD's dinner is more than twenty-five minutes overdue. As you know, he needs comestibles according to his preset canine dining plan.

"Basically, *Wolf Wanderer,* I don't know what you all were expecting our poor peckish PugNaut to do. The little guy is hungry, for gosh sakes! America is watching! The *world* is watching! We don't need NASA to get a bad reputation with PETA! Clean up the cabin and feed PD immediately!

"Houston out!"

Avoiding the four pairs of glaring eyes shooting daggers my (Hungry! Empty-bellied! This-close-to-messaging PETA!) way, I leap up a few inches and grab the floating scoop in my maw and gleefully glide over to generally smiley Roger, hopeful that he might find the funny in all this.

He takes my dinner dipper and forces a small smile.

"PD?" he says as he grabs, one by one, what I assume are the 27 to 30 kibble pieces that researcher Roger allocated for my meals from the air around us. "Let's get you fed and to bed and hope that tomorrow, the only brown thing flying around the ship is a squirrel!"

My belly and heart sing. *Fed* and *squirrels* in the same sentence! All in all, a great day. Clearly, nothing else can go wrong for America's beloved PugNaut. . . .

WW
MISSION
FOOD
FOOD
DRINKS
DRINKS
CONDIMENTS
CONDIMENTS
FOOD
FOOD
DRINKS
CONDIMENTS
UTENSILS
KIBBLE BIN TWO
KIBBLE BIN ONE
KIBBLE BIN THREE

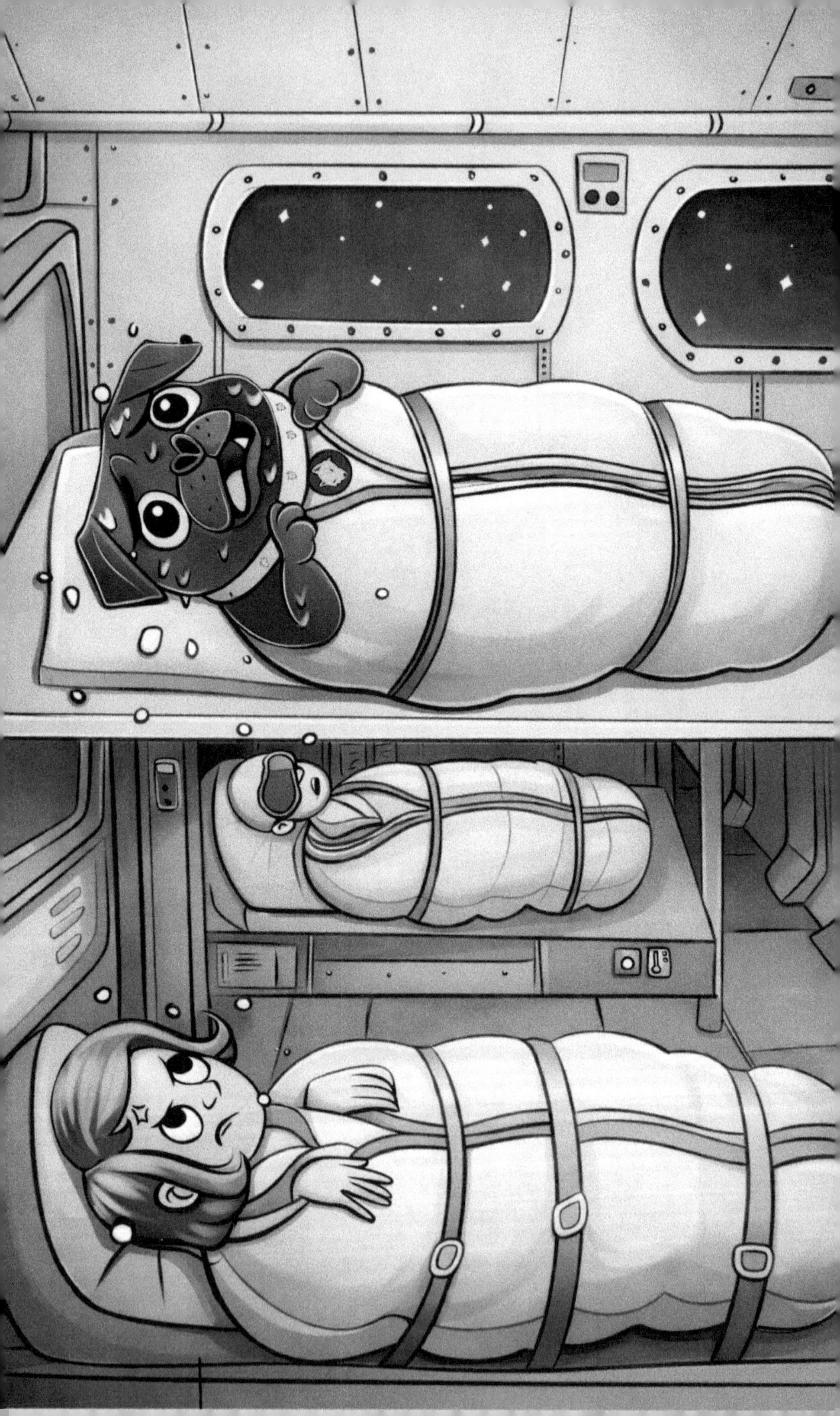

Chapter Three

IN SPACE, NO ONE CAN HEAR YOU BARK

The Rogers have put me in a straitjacket.

It has been an hour since what my space mates dubbed "PD's kibble catastrophe." One minute I was hearing them say it was time for bed, and the next thing I knew I was tightly zipped up in a pug-sized wrap and tethered to the wall.

I've never felt more constrained, curbed, crimped or cramped. If Ralph were here, I'd be sunk.

Someone help me! Someone save me! Someone get me out of here!

I paw as hard as I can against the constricting fabric as it occurs to me I'm likely being held here as they prepare a padded cell. Mommy calls me her "crazy little dog" when she thinks I'm acting up, but I never thought this day would come.

The wrap is damp with my sweat as I try with all my pug might to claw my way free. *Alas,* I think as the wetness around makes me thankful for the potty break my captors allowed before placing me in this pug prison, *I am stuck, stuck, stuck, stuck, stuck. . . .*

"PD? PD! You're snuffling and snarling and snorting!" snaps a very annoyed Rogerette from what appears to be her own blue straitjacket that is tethered below mine.

My scared eyes roam around the cabin to my other crewmates (*captors!*), who for some reason—did unfriendly aliens sneak on board?—are likewise trapped. But, unlike me, they don't look scared to be in straitjackets. *Why? Why aren't they terrified too?* my panicked mind screams as I attempt to shake some sweat off my damp nose. *Why is no one else all afeared and affrighted about being imprisoned?* The last time I was this panicked was when that huge mastiff kept licking my whole face at doggie daycare.

"Houston to *Wolf Wanderer*, Houston to *Wolf Wanderer*," comes the familiar voice of Administrator Jetson over the comm, waking the rest of the (trapped!) crew. "We are picking up a large amount of liquid circulating around the sleeping area. Shall I engage the flood stoppage equipment?"

"Heh-heh, no need, Houston," giggles a sleepy-but-cheerful smiley Roger. "It's just our perspiring pug, PD. Apparently the little guy thought we put him in the hoosegow instead of his little hammock. All is okay here on *Wolf Wanderer*!"

"Roger! Please be sure not to overfeed him tomorrow before commencing the experiments. Houston out!"

Despite already feeling famished upon learning it won't be an all-PD-can-eat kibble buffet tomorrow morning, I'm glad that at least the frenzied, fear-filled ferret that has been racing around my brain has departed. In my calmer state, I now recall Mommy reading from our information packet that astronauts sleep in special bedrolls that are designed to keep the sleeper in place and create the snug, cocoon-like feel normally provided by gravity.

Too bad, because now I have no my excuse for my freak-out.

"There seems to be excessive humidity in our spacecraft due to the multitude of droplets emanating from PD's bedroll," observes egghead Roger from his bedroll. "This level of apprehension and agitation might lead to his having an involuntary loss of bladder control.

"I didn't think PD would need to be fitted in a Maximum Absorbency Garment, but perhaps I was in error."

"No, he's fine; it's just a normal canine reaction to restraint," opines researcher Roger. "My pug personality study said PD should be expected to exhibit panic, anxiety and trepidation the first night in his sleeping bag. Dogs don't like to feel smothered and bound."

Smiley Roger, likely noting my confused countenance, grins at me. "Lucky you, little buddy! No doggie diaper,"—here he catches the glare from egghead Roger—"er, Maximum Absorbency Garment for you yet! But if you do a space stroll,"—another scowl from highbrow Roger—"er, Extra-Vehicular Activity, you'll need to be all Pampered up!"

Huh? Dog Pampers? Strolling out there in space? Nobody told me any of this! I don't want to wear diapers! I don't know how to do a walkie in space! There isn't any oxygen! I will poopie my nappie while I suffocate! I want to go home! I want Mommy! I want Mommy! I . . .

"PD!! Stop wriggling and jiggling! I am trying to sleep!" yells a drowsy, displeased Rogerette as she peels away her sleep mask and glowers at me. "Your bed is jouncing all over the place, and if you don't calm down you are going to thresh and thrash your way right out of your bag and . . ."

Oops. Too late.

Apparently my inner anxious, antsy wolf wants to wander the *Wolf Wanderer* and won't be denied. Running wolves reportedly can reach speeds nearly forty miles per hour, and I'm ready to test that theory. The next thing I know, I've wriggled my furry fanny out of my sleep sack and succumbed not only to a zag of the zoomies but . . .

Zero! Gravity! Zoomies!

"Saucer-eyed" is the most apt way to describe my space mates as they watch me bounce around the spacecraft's sleeping area, careening and caroming off walls, columns, tables, ceiling, floor and all four Rogers, who hurriedly unzip and exit their bedrolls and take cover behind any object that might shield them from this frenzied, frantic flying fur ball.

I ricochet and rebound, boomerang and buck, spin and spring, all the while whacking my stout self over and over into cabinets and closets and containers. Rogerette's lightning-like reflexes are the sole reason I don't fly into the instrument panel, which for all I know could have altered our course and sent us to Uranus or some such. My paws whap any and every object that's not tied down as Space Storm PD swirls and swoops and soars.

In my mind's eye, I am in a race with dozens of ghosts of zoomies past. I am under the zoomies' spell, hypnotized and seduced and entranced, with no control over my whirligigging and whooshing and whizzing. *No control! No restraint! Rushing and racing and running and . . .*

Smack!

I snap out of my trance as I collide with the hardcover copy of *Pug Personality Manual* that researcher Roger is holding like a shield to block my zigzagging path. The impact has the effect of turning off the PD pinball machine. Cartoon stars orbit my hard head; I think I hear those cartoon birds too but probably not because I'm pretty sure they can't fly this high. Too bad, since maybe I could have pointed a paw their way and given the Rogers my best "I didn't do it, Mommy" look of angelic innocence.

Alas, the eight orbs stink-eyeing me don't instill much hope for absolution. In fact, the quartet of scowls has me wishing I were back in my sleeping bag—only with the opening zipped all the way shut, resembling the straitjacket I thought I was in in the first place.

I chance a glance around the spacecraft to see what's causing all this glaring and glowering. *Uh-oh. Not good, PD, not good.* For as far as my bulging orbs can see, our space home resembles an Airbnb just vacated by a fraternity. As I peek around, I am reminded of the mesmerizing strength of the zoomies. Once under its spell, I am powerless and paralyzed. Surely my mates will absolve me of prosecution and punishment. I mean, look—my googlies may have been open whilst I sped and sprinted, but, I assure you, nobody was home.

I'm astounded (and, okay, maybe a wee bit impressed) by the degree of the chaos I wrought. Pretty much everything that wasn't bolted down—and some things that were in closed containers—are floating about. Obviously *someone* crashed into—and opened—cabinets, boxes, bins, and every other type of storage container. So! Much! Stuff!

"PD? I can only assume this deviation from sane behavior is due to what the *Pug Personality Manual* refers to as Frenetic Random Activity Periods," researcher Roger opines as he and my other crewmates stop frowning at me and start to set aright all that I set so very wrong while possessed by the zoomies. "We know you likely have a lot of pent-up energy and stress due to the demands of being America's first canine in space. But this midnight madness, this scrumbling and scrambling cannot continue!"

Chastised, I turn toward Rogerette, who is at the white-board where she has written "Zoomies Aftermath Cleaning Assignments," under which she is listing each spacecraft area and which is to be neatened by whom. Being pretty much an anti-chore dog, I am sore at the idea of helping with the tidying up (despite being the reason for our playing this middle-of-the-night maid game). Then she writes "PD" next to "Kitchen and Pantry."

Ooh! Wait! I love this game, I decide, snagglegrinning over my assignment as my suddenly grumbling belly reminds me that a bout of the zoomies burns a lot of calories. *I could do with a bit of a nosh right about now,* I think, and as the others stare at the whiteboard, I stare into the distance, imagining myself getting into Kibble Bin One—more carefully this time!—and swiping a kibble or two (or ten).

"Listen up, everybody," egghead Roger calls over his shoulder as he waves around a small box that formerly housed the now-airborne DVDs, then starts arm-swimming toward the den. "It is one in the morning. I know PD has caused quite a lot of clutter. But if we focus, we can have everything back in its proper place within the hour. We're all exhausted, and we need to be well rested for our first day of experiments."

I know that latter word is meant to remind me that tomorrow is a big day, but I can't worry about that right now. I have more important things bouncing about my brain. Okay, one thing bouncing about. My favorite thing: food!

A quick peek at my space colleagues lets me know I can push off for the pantry without drawing eyes. Plus, unlike yesterday's foray into the food area, I am *assigned* there this time. So hopefully the crew is more into straightening up and then getting straight back to bed than wondering what PD on KP is getting up to.

I enter the kitchen, lingering aloft a moment as I consider whether I should tidy up or dine first, and then I slap a paw across my maw to stifle the guffaw that nearly escapes. *As if it's a contest,* I laugh inwardly. *As if a pug has the ability to place anything above eating!*

Lucky for me, my whirlwind through this area apparently was brief. There are a bunch of condiments floating around, as well as cutlery, plates and bowls, a few mugs, and a cookbook titled *Heavenly Eating in the Heavens.* But amazingly there is no food floating about, meaning my zoom-zoom through here didn't involve a quick bite.

Which is a bummer, as it would be nice if food were already airborne and at the ready. No matter; it's not like I am uneducated in how to get into the kibble containers. I risk one more peek from the kitchen/pantry and see Rogerette hard at it in the den and smiley Roger hurriedly neatening tomes and pads and pens in the experiment space. *All clear!*

I do a happy ballerina spin—okay, more Hyacinth Hippo from Walt Disney's *Fantasia* than prima ballerina Anna Pavlova—and gleefully make my way toward my old friend Kibble Bin One. I stare at the lid, suddenly overcome with hunger as I imagine a plummeting blood sugar level due to no nummies since dinner. I know I have to do this unlatching trick more slowly this go-round and find a way around the no-thumbs problem that led to yesterday's food fiasco.

Flipping my squat self upside down, I press my forepaws on the lid to keep the bin from flying open and again causing a kibble cascade. That done, I use my short snout to unfasten the side snap and very slowly, very carefully, very calmly . . .

No! Not again!

Tiny golden-brown spherical pieces of yum waft upward as Kibble Bin One sends its palate-pleasing payload into the pantry and—unless I think of something quick!—beyond. I frantically bat my paws at the floating food, trying in vain to steer it back to its bin home. But it's no use; I'm winded after getting maybe four little pieces back in the container. I remember hearing Mommy telling someone that she read there are fourteen cups of kibble in my four-pound food bag, so I can't even guess how many morsels are doing their slow-motion swirl around me now.

Lord. I didn't realize kitchen clean-up would include a hoovering. Good thing I'm a food-vacuuming pro.

Opening my jaw wider than a newborn bird anticipating its first worm, I paddle my little legs from one kibble to the next, pretending I'm that video game icon Pac-Man and imitating his "wokka-wokka-wokka" noise as I *chomp! chomp! chomp!* and try to clear the maze of the dots, er, clear the air of the kibble. I rarely feel full, but after ten minutes of inhaling chow I feel uncharacteristically bloated. Surely the room is nearly free of dog food, because . . .

Crud, I think, as I dare a glance around me. *I haven't made a dent.* There must be a million billion ka trillion pieces to go. Fighting discouragement, I smack my noggin with my paw. *Get it together, PD!* I admonish myself. *You're an embarrassment to PugDom! Eat! Eat up this mess!*

I redouble my effort, re-open my wide mouth, and return to my noshtest. I gobble and gulp, munch and masticate, gnaw and gnash. My belly feels like the foil over a pan of Jiffy Pop, each piece of kibble another kernel popping and pushing outward, outward, outward . . .

The final floating kibble bit drifts toward my mouth. Just as smiley Roger pokes his head into the pantry to check my progress, I suck it in, swallow and loudly belch.

"Holy moly, PD! You startled me!" he chuckles before inspecting the progress I've made on tidying the zippy zoomer–upended, still *very* messy room. Then, for what might be the first time ever, he actually frowns. "Uh . . . whatcha been doing for the past thirty minutes, little buddy? No offense, but . . . it is almost two in the morning, and we all need to get some shut-eye before taking on tomorrow's experiment. Here, let me help you."

His smile returns as he begins returning items to their rightful containers, cases and canisters. I try and help, but, Lord, I'm moving like my Uncle Clayton after a Thanksgiving feast. I'm just so full, and there is no way I could fit in even one more bite, because . . .

"Hey, PD, looks like you broke open the peanut butter Pooch Creamery dog ice cream. It's kinda melty . . . might as well give you some before sticking it back in the fridge, right?"

So right! I think, grinning my gleamiest snaggletooth at smiley Roger, who's already dishing a spoonful into my dog dish. I take my time lapping it in—hard as that is for a pug—since eating is a lot more enjoyable than helping with chores. I lick the last drop from the rim just as whistle-while-you-work Roger closes the last open case and then scrutinizes his job. He's just about to usher us out when his eyes fall on . . .

The wide-open, empty Kibble Bin One.

The smile on his face now is more like a confused grin, one corner up, one down. He turns to me to find me shaking my head, shrugging my withers, beaming full-on snaggle and just trying to appear innocent of any food crime. But then I espy the camera in the corner . . . and I slap my paws over my ears as the one voice I didn't want to hear booms through the comms:

"Houston to *Wolf Wanderer*! Houston to *Wolf Wanderer*!"

Busted.

Houston to Wolf Wanderer!
Houston to Wolf Wanderer!
NASA
WW MISSION
NASA

Experiment One

Pug Rodent Pursuit

Chapter Four

PAVLOV'S (PUG) DOG

I salivate just thinking about food.

So, I have to say: That Russian physiologist Ivan Pavlov was on to something with his experiments with dogs in the 1890s. His discovery of what now is known as "classical conditioning" came from measuring dogs' saliva when he gave them food while he simultaneously rang a bell. Over time, the dogs would salivate when the bell sounded regardless of whether food was present.

I get it. Anything that reminds dogs of dining brings on the drool.

And that is why, as I await the start of *Wolf Wanderer* experiment one, I am practically frothing at the mouth just imagining the squirrel that soon will be mine.

I mean, not that I have ever actually *eaten* a squirrel. But I sure have chased them lots of times! Wait, that's not true either. But only because the Warden, a.k.a. Mommy, keeps a tight hold on my leash during walkies in case I see a squirrel and try to tear free of her to catch it.

So I am as giddy as it gets now, hovering above the research table that my space mates secured me to a few minutes ago before they went to set up today's test. I haven't been told much, other than it's called *Pug Rodent Pursuit in Zero Gravity: Implications for Advancements in Olympic and Other Athletic Training.*

Obviously the naming assignment was given to egghead Roger. I have neither clue nor interest in what the goal of this experiment is. I'm sure it's crucial and vital and important and of mega-consequence to the very survival of man- and dogkind.

Just. Get. The. Squirrel. Already.

As I await the start of the test, I imagine bringing my captured space squirrel home to Mommy so she can cook it for me. *That Google man says squirrels can be stewed, fried or even cooked on a spit. They supposedly taste like rabbit or the dark meat of chicken. I read that a single squirrel can yield one or two pounds of meat after Mommy skins it and stuff. Especially in Fall, when squirrels are all nice and fattened up! And I really like food a lot, and so having a lot means . . .*

"PD? Please stop dripping your drool all over the research table! There are important papers secured to it that we need," Rogerette yips at me as she air-swims into the area to grab a large box. She stares at me a moment, then adds as she carries the box back to the testing team: "Relax a few minutes, PD. You'll need your energy for today's test, okay?"

Energy from where? I inwardly gripe as I think of this morning's paltry portion of kibble. Sadly, the crew did not override Administrator Jetson's "underfeed PD" directive. So my kibble allotment left me unsatisfied to say the least. Apparently, I need to be alert and ready to race and not in full-tummy ready-for-naptime mode when the squirrel gets here.

Speaking of which . . . *Where Is It?*

I summon some patience by reminding myself that I'm lucky I even get to do the experiment at all. Last night, when the camera caught a certain pug getting into and scarfing down every single morsel in Kibble Bin One, and then Administrator Jetson's, er, *ever-so-slightly* disappointed and displeased voice boomed over the comm . . . well, I was scared I was about to be drifting out in space à la George Clooney in *Gravity* or something.

"PD, I am sure there is a good reason you were gobbling and gulping pilfered kibble instead of cleaning the kitchen area, but I find this conduct unbecoming of America's first spacedog," the administrator had admonished me before suddenly softening and redirecting his attention from me to the Rogers.

"But wait. Crew? Did you frighten little PD with tales of the small breakfast he was to get before the testing? If you traumatized the poor little pug, then who could blame him if his fear of forthcoming famine perhaps awoke some ancestral need to hurriedly find food?"

Before my gobsmacked teammates could offer a defense, he added—to my disappointment, I might add—"PD, I am sorry to say that a small breakfast *will* be necessary to ensure motivation for the first test, but I am sure you won't even notice once the engaging, exciting test is underway.

"Now! Everyone please get back to bed! Houston out!"

I looked anywhere but at what I imagined was a very frowny foursome as they in unison signed off with a "*Wolf Wanderer* out!" and then slowly turned their way to hear my expected lecture. Amazingly, the group merely shook its collective head and, after re-securing me in my sleep sack, went nighty-nigh.

So now it's around ten the next morning. The test was supposed to start at eight but Administrator Jetson let us sleep in a little since we were up so late cleaning. Of course, one of us didn't sleep that well because he was too wound up over a certain squirrel he was soon to chase! And every time I finally did fall asleep I would dream of catching him!

As the clock tick-tick-ticks with no humans or squirrels yet to be seen in the research area, I try and mellow my mania by thinking of other things. *Other things. Other things. Other things . . .*

There are *no other things! There is only the squirrel!*

Just as I am thinking I might need a straitjacket after all, Rogerette comes into the room carrying the box I'd seen her leave with earlier. I pay her and her parcel little mind as she sets it down and then turns to watch her colleagues come in behind her. Frustration builds in me as I note that none of the Rogers is burdened with a squirrel cage. I am starting to fret that NASA forgot to pack the rodent and the test is off. *This day is ruined! It's all ruined!*

But just as the song in my heart dies, the box seems to come to life.

Chirp! Bark! Screech! I startle and whip my head to the noise-emitting container and then to egghead Roger, who is pressing buttons on a remote control he just pulled from his pocket. Then, smiley Roger, looking uncharacteristically serious, very slowly opens the box and scoops out the packing peanuts that I bet the squirrel wishes were real peanuts and carefully puts them in a bag so they don't go airborne like *someone's* kibble. Next, researcher Roger glides to the whiteboard and, under the title of today's test, writes *Step 1: Introduce PD to NutJob.*

Huh? Who?

"PD, meet NutJob!" exclaims now-laughing smiley Roger as he lifts what appears to be a stuffed animal—albeit a chirping, chattering stuffed animal—out of the box and holds it close to my surprised and confused face. "NutJob, meet PD!"

Oh, very funny, gang, but I'm on to you, I smirk at them all as I decide I am being punked. I glance around looking for the cosmic ghost of Allen Funt, the man who in 1948 started his long-running hidden camera, practical joke reality television series, *Candid Camera.* Alas, no Mr. Funt apparition appears.

But as I stare at the rodent in smiley Roger's hands, it occurs to me that there is something otherworldly about it. I mean, like it's a squirrel but sorta not a squirrel. And then it hits me. Smiley Roger is *not* holding a stuffed squirrel.

Smiley Roger is holding a *ROBOT SQUIRREL*. And there's nothing smiley about it! How can I compete with a mechanically enhanced rodent?

I am about to grab the nearest escape pod and race home to Mommy when it occurs to me: NASA wouldn't choose a squirrel-squeamish scaredy-dog to be America's first-ever dognaut! *Pug up, PD!* I think, calling upon courage I sure don't feel. *Squash that squirrel Squelch that squirrel Squish that squirrel Squander that squirrel Squ—*

"PD? Don't you wanna meet the competition?" says Rogerette, nodding toward smiley Roger, who, during my internal PD pep talk, floated right next to me and is now holding a very crazed-looking, chirping, wriggling "NutJob" about two inches from my flat snout. I flinch, trying not to go into an embarrassing cower, as I take in this faux-fur-covered metal monstrosity that I am about to try and catch.

The rodent looks both fabricated and all too authentic:

- Its beady eyes—not black, but rather a demonic crimson—focus unwaveringly on me without blinking, like the evil stare of a doll in a horror movie combined with the up-all-night manic look of a drugged-up alley dweller.
- Its red-brown fur is somehow fluffy and soft-looking despite being synthetic.
- Its bushy tail, controlled by the remote whose buttons egghead Roger gleefully presses, flicks back and forth

slowly and menacingly as if at any moment it will propel the monster right at my quivering body.

- The structure under its factory-made coat looks Goliath-solid, the silky outer covering belying the warrior underneath, taunting would-be pursuers with the illusion that it's nothing more than easily overcome prey. But under its dense, fine, pettable pelt, it's constructed of thick metal, fitted out with intricate springs, gears, wires, functional joints and moving parts.
- Its small pointy ears waggle at me as it likely interprets the pounding of my pug heart—correctly!—as terror. Its wiggly nose likely detects my dread. Its metallic claws appear formed of the sharpest steel and ready to grab and grip any foe.
- But the teeth! *Lord almighty, the teeth!* Cartoonishly long, razor-sharp and formidably strong, the orange-brown faux enamel monstrosities look ready to make easy prey of nuts . . . tree bark . . . me. *Me!*

Where is the escape pod? Where is the escape pod? Where is the escape pod?!

I try and fail to look courageous, completely forgetting the motivational speech I just gave myself as my round head shakes *No! No! No!* and my wide eyes frantically dart in every direction, seeking a way out of this trial. Just as I feel a faint coming on, researcher Roger buys me some time, raising a finger as he picks up *The Pug Personality Manual.*

“Gang, we need to give PD a moment to get acquainted with NutJob. The manual says pugs thrive on companionship and are generally adaptable to new experiences and situations, but when introducing a pug to new stimuli you should give him a moment to process the object or being.

“Hmmm,” he adds, studying the page in front of him. “The guide says PD’s curious nature means he likely will accept NutJob; however, it mentions that sudden alterations to circumstances can evoke feelings of disquiet and angst. But, given that PD was screened for bravery in any and all conditions and for capacity to accommodate new items being added to his environment . . .”

“Ah-oooooooooo! Ah-oooooooooo! Ah-oooooooooo!”

The deep, rumbling wail that comes out of me causes all the Rogers to jump a bit, as far as an astronaut can jump in zero gravity. They look around for the source of what sounds like a lovelorn ghoul haunting a graveyard.

Smiley Roger quickly places the faux squirrel back in its box. “Take a few minutes to compose yourself, little buddy,” he says, scratching me behind ears pulled tightly back as I whimper and yowl. “America’s first dog in space ain’t afraid of no squirrel!”

I’m about to relinquish my place in the history books when Administrator Jetson’s voice thunders through the comm:

“Houston to *Wolf Wanderer*! Houston to *Wolf Wanderer*!”

“Go ahead, Houston.”

"*Wolf Wanderer*, what is that infernal noise? All of us at Mission Control had to turn down the volume on our headsets just now! What *is* that? Sounds like an actual wolf is aboard *Wolf Wanderer*!"

Egghead Roger gives me a "Zip it, PD!" glare and then waits for me to stop whining and keening before replying.

"Apologies to the base crew, Houston. That reverberating ululation you heard was simply the primal cry of a mammal about to vanquish his foe. PD momentarily became one with his brave ancestors when he was introduced to his rodent adversary. He's back to his dognaut self now, though. All's well here, Administrator."

As Administrator Jetson signs off, I am about to do the Snoopy dance for escaping a lecture from the big boss when I note four very unhappy-looking Rogers glowering my way. They look at one another and then back to me before Rogerette grits her teeth, takes a deep breath and speaks for the group.

"PD . . .," she begins, narrowing her eyes behind glasses she has moved down her nose so that her glaring eyes appear cartoon-large, sorta like the old-time Looney Tunes cartoon episode when that yellow canary named Tweety put on glasses and his eyes were *gigantic*. Except Rogerette isn't funny like Tweety. No one here is laughing like they would if she were Tweety.

"PD, you need to hear me very clearly. The success of the *Wolf Wanderer* mission—and, by extension, the decision of whether the four of us remain employed by NASA—is largely dependent on the success of the experiments we were assigned to complete. And that means the experiments led by dognaut PD the Pug. And *that* means that if you don't buckle down and prepare for—and successfully complete—this and the other tests: We. Could. Lose. Our. Jobs."

Chastised, I look away from her hardened, squinting eyes and stare at my reflection in the window of the spaceship. *You can do this, PD!* I tell myself, feigning bravery. *You can't send astronauts to the unemployment line! Get it together!*

"Showtime, Squirrel Conqueror!" laughs smiley Roger as he leashes NutJob to one of two research tables and egghead Roger leashes me to the other. "Let's see who's the predator and who's the prey!"

Just as I'm feeling a bit miffed at this seeming lack of confidence in my easy victory over the mutant squirrel, researcher Roger, back at his whiteboard, taps the dry-erase marker at the notations he has added since writing the title and the meet-and-greet step. My eyes likely resemble the soccer ball–sized ones of the colossal squid—which reportedly measure eleven inches in diameter—as I read:

Step 2: Fit PD with blinders

Step 3: Fit PD with flippers

Step 4: Reset stopwatch

Step 5: Explain chase rules to PD

Step 6: Release NutJob and choose "Prey" program on remote

Step 7: Start stopwatch

Step 8: When PD tags the target, stop the stopwatch and record the time

Step 9: Repeat test two more times and note PD's best time

Researcher Roger waits for everyone to read over the steps before reaching for a container labelled SQUIRREL EXPERIMENT EQUIPMENT. All the other Rogers are patiently floating about, watching as the blinders and flippers are removed from the box. Smiley Roger reaches over to take hold of my collar and bring me to egghead Roger when he notes something seems off . . .

"Whoa, guys," he exclaims as he stares into what heretofore were my brown googlies but which now likely appear mostly white. "I think PD is about to faint."

All four Rogers now are swirling around me. Or I think they are. Maybe my head is swirling all around and I just think my teammates are swirling. I don't know. The last thing I remember is something about a robotic monster squirrel with scary fangs and scary claws and something about having to wear something that makes me blind while I flip around as he eats me. I hate this game.

"You okay, PD?" Rogerette asks, rubbing my back in an apparent attempt to bring me back to the present moment. "Nothing to fear, brave dognaut. You're just going to wear a few items that will positively influence and improve the test results."

Improve? For whom? I fret to myself. *For the squirrel, maybe! I'm the one who'll be blind and in flip-flops while the nefarious NutJob prepares to dine on the dog! I thought this was a chase game! I thought I was just going to catch my first squirrel, not be devoured by it! I hate this game! I hate this game! I . . .*

"PD? PD, please drop that flipper from your mouth and pay attention," says an exasperated-looking researcher Roger. "You of course are wondering what these implements are for and what the test is all about. So, before we unleash NutJob, let me explain the rules so you feel calm and prepared. And don't fret—NutJob's creators programmed the rules into his cyber brain so he understands the test's directives."

Oh please, I snort. *I'll bet those demon teeth won't be following rules!*

"First, you needn't fear the blinders; they won't make you blind but will merely narrow your field of vision a bit so you can focus on the chase and not be distracted by objects around you. See, pugs have a wider field of vision than humans. We see approximately 180 degrees while you see more like 250 degrees. That's because your eyes are positioned more towards the sides of your head, see, and . . ."

But I've tuned him out.

Because my 250-degree field of vision is focused on something out there in the ginormous universe beyond the thick windows of our spaceship: Sirius the Dog Star, the brightest star in the whole night sky! That space book Mommy read to me said Sirius is in the constellation Canis Major, which just so *happens* to mean "greater dog" in Latin. And Sirius is talking to me! *Me!* And I know he is saying, "Be brave, little PD! You can beat a silly squirrel! After all, there's no Squirrel Star! But there's a Dog Star!"

PD is Dog Star Junior! PD is Dog Star Junior! PD is . . .

"So anyway . . ."

I snap to and turn from the window back to researcher Roger, who's still droning on about fields of vision. "You can see more around you than we humans can without even turning your head. So we need to limit that a bit so you can stay completely focused on NutJob."

As I peer about for that scary scamp of a squirrel, Rogerette drifts over with the three flippers I didn't try to eat and takes the still slightly soggy one back from the egghead Roger, who has been holding it since snatching it out of my mouth.

"PD," begins Rogerette, taking my left forepaw in one hand and placing a flipper on it with the other, "NASA wants to see if wearing flippers will help you in your pursuit of NutJob. Research on human swimmers shows that flippers enhance performance by increasing propulsion and improving kicking technique.

"So the idea is that they might help you push against zero gravity better, maybe helping you cover a larger area more quickly—sorta like if you were swimming, see?"

Well, no, I *don't* see because I am *averse to swimming*. In fact, when Mommy and I go to James Hunter Dog Park near our house in Arlington, I get scared just looking at the little swim area! Pugs have a brachycephalic airway, which means I have a shorter snout and narrowed nasal passages and also

I have a round body and short legs and I get tired and . . . *LOOK, DO YOU WANT ME TO DROWN?*

Over at the whiteboard, researcher Roger is tap-tap-tapping his dry-erase marker against the board again in an impatient, annoyed manner. He has just made a checkmark by the "flippers" step after noting I'm now outfitted in all four rubber swim shoes.

"Okay, okay, we're getting behind," he grouses while twirling his hand at smiley Roger, indicating it's time to hook the leather blinder straps around my little ears and position them to the outside of each bulging eye. Smiley Roger nods and floats over to retrieve the blinders, and within moments my peripheral vision shrinks so much that I fear NutJob—*and his teeth!*—will be able to attack from almost any angle without my having any warning.

Clad in my blinders and flippers, I do my best to face the whiteboard at an angle that lets me see most of it. Researcher Roger is holding a stopwatch aloft and is again spinning his other hand at smiley Roger.

"PD," he says, turning toward me, "it's time for your first experiment. We are going to unleash both you and NutJob. Then we are going to start the stopwatch and simultaneously activate NutJob's 'Prey' mode on his remote, which tells his robotic squirrel brain that he is going to be pursued and should try and avoid capture. Your job is to 'catch' your prey, but for our purposes you need only touch any part of him for your effort to be considered successful. We will do the pursuit three times and record our findings.

"Got it?" he asks, staring into my shaded eyeballs.

Well, no, I most certainly do not "got it," I fume. *I thought I was going to actually catch—and dominate! defeat! destroy!—my first squirrel. What is this "touch" nonsense? No! This is not what I signed up for! No, no, no! Because I thought . . .*

"GO!" yells Rogerette as my nemesis is unleashed by egghead Roger and I am freed by researcher Roger and the stopwatch starts ticking.

The next thing I know, I am on a levitating stage, strobe lights spinning and disco music playing as the four Rogers dance like extras in Saturday Night Fever. *Administrator Jetson appears in person thanks to our* Star Trek *transporter, his molecules reuniting after his seconds-long trip from Houston. He is weeping with pride after watching me trap NutJob in empty Kibble Bin One a mere minute into the chase, and he is pinning a medal to my collar that reads Champion Canine. NutJob, held captive in the kibble container, is the only one not celebrating my stunning performance.*

Er, wait. Let's try again:

The next thing I know, I am somehow locked inside empty Kibble Bin One. NutJob's chattering, chittering teeth are clacking in what I can only assume is a robot squirrel song of triumph. The first test pretty much consisted of my trying to find forward momentum as the flippers had me spinning wildly in circles, thudding, thwacking, ramming and whamming into any and all surfaces and obstacles in my path. As I rapidly reeled, NutJob grabbed me with his metal claws, halting my gyrations before taking my collar in his fangs and—in a reversal of our prey-pursuer roles—carrying me to the kitchen, where he unlocked the food bin and swatted me therein with his big bushy bristly tail.

Oh, and Administrator Jetson did not make an appearance. Unless you count his voice, now rumbling over the comm.

"Houston to *Wolf Wanderer*. Houston to *Wolf Wanderer* . . ."

"Go ahead, Houston," I hear Rogerette respond as she opens the bin to free me.

"Have you all clearly explained the experiment's parameters to PD?" our boss asks, sounding both disappointed and concerned. "I'm worried he was not informed of who is the hunter and who is the huntee. . . .

"You all have two more chances to test his pursuit skills. Please be aware that NASA is hoping to use the results of this and the other tests to give America a big step up in athletics—particularly the Olympics—propelling us ahead of all other nations. I do realize that that's a large onus to place on PD's little back, but we are counting on his teammates to help him to, at a *minimum*, understand his assignment!

"Now then, get PD out of the kibble bin and back to the research room for round two! Houston out!"

As Rogerette lassos NutJob and motions for me to air-swim behind her and that demonic rodent back to the research room, I avoid her stink eye and instead offer a prayer to God and a plea to the Dog Star, asking for courage. Because I can't bear to lose to that nefarious noxious NutJob again! I have to win! I have to help athletes and dogkind (and NASA)!

"Okay, guys!" researcher Roger says, clapping his hands like my old trainer Miss Sophia used to do to get my attention. "Hurry up and leash Pursuer PD and Prey NutJob to the tables. The pug book says pugs do better at tasks as they repeat them, so I think he will be successful this go-round."

Thanks, Sirius, for somehow making my colleague believe in me, I think smilingly. *I know I am going to be remembered as the famous dognaut whose prowess and mastery over his space tests led to leaps in science, medicine, academia and product development. History books will devote entire chapters to me. Children will study me in school. Documentaries will tell generations to come of my contributions . . .*

"GO!" roars Rogerette. NutJob and I are simultaneously untethered as the dreaded stopwatch again starts ticking.

Thankfully this round goes splendidly.

As my central nervous system grasps how to air-swim like Flipper the Dolphin with my flippers, I easily keep pace with my quarry while also managing to avoid upending a single item as I dart and dash around the spacecraft. My blinders pose zero sight limitations due to my mastery over how best to tilt my head and rotate my neck to achieve a nearly panoramic view of the area. My barrel chest puffs up beyond what I would have thought possible as our second lap around the spaceship culminates in my first-ever capture of a rodent. NutJob, weary from the chase, barely offers up resistance; his fur-covered metal forearms make a last-ditch effort to scratch my belly as I squeeze my strong hind legs around his head and fly us over to my old friend Kibble Bin One and imprison him therein.

Tears of joy spring to my eyes as I hear champagne corks popping over the comm as the Mission Control people whoop and hoot.

From somewhere far off in the cosmos, I hear Sirius the Dog Star admonishing me to be a truthful dognaut. So, let me try again . . .

I imagine Flipper the Dolphin making his characteristic whistles and clicks as he explains how to pilot around a spacecraft in scuba shoes, but it's no use; two minutes into the chase, my twirls and whirls have led to a doubling of the amount of items I'll be re-shelving, re-boxing and replacing this evening. My left blinder, during one particularly swirly swivel, has flopped over so that my entire orb is blocked, the point driven home when my enemy's feared fangs chomp! on my curly tail. I try and fail to catch sight of NutJob through my partial view from the right side, but it's almost as if his robot brain knows I'm half blind and so he mounts a full-scale attack from my left. Bite! Scratch! Screech! I try to defend myself, but alas, I'm a vision-impaired, swimming-impaired, central nervous system–impaired pug. And moments later, I get a one-eyed view of the inside of Kibble Bin One as the lid is slammed shut by that malevolent monster.

So basically no champagne. No whoops. No hoots. Just blackness and near-silence, broken only by the maddening, buzz-saw-from-Hades clicking and clacking of those mutant teeth.

From the bottom of the kibble bin, I wallow in shame and disgrace, fearing I so blew the first test that I am about to be booted right out of *Wolf Wanderer*, sentenced to forever wander the heavens alone, shunned even by my former bestie, Sirius. I see myself floating away into the void;

I envisage Administrator Jetson, his brows heavy over his sad eyes, disillusion and disappointment etched into his expression; I imagine the four Rogers disgraced as they clear out their NASA lockers, then glum and gloomy as they dispiritedly go through job listing sites . . . thanks to PD, thanks to PD, thanks to PD . . .

"PD? Buddy?"

I tilt my head up and to the right so that that eye can sort of make out smiley Roger, who is floating above the food bin.

"Chin up, PD! Three's a charm, right?" As he reaches into the bin and lifts me out, I stare at him with my uni-orb, wondering how someone about to be unemployed thanks to me can maintain a happy countenance.

Smiley Roger and I rejoin the rest of the Rogers in the research room, all of them gathered around my nemesis NutJob who again is tethered to a table. As I near him and am leashed to my own table, I sense his squirrel brain circuits somehow computing that he has just one more chase to go before declaring victory. His chilling choppers chew at the air; his nightmarish nails knead the tabletop; his eerie eyes seem focused afar as if they already see me again imprisoned in the kibble container.

Well, I guess everyone truly is getting canned, I think as fear again overtakes me. But just as I am about expose my pug belly in the common canine sign of surrender, I suddenly imagine my Dog Star mentor peering in the window of *Wolf Wanderer*, looking right into my very soul, and saying, "Use the Force, PD! The Dog Force is with you . . ."

"GO!" shouts Rogerette as my adversary is unleashed by egghead Roger and I am freed by researcher Roger and the stopwatch sounds a loud *Tink!*

The last thing I remember is locking my pug googly orbs to the squirrel's evil eyes and thinking, *You're mine, you reprobate rodent! Mine!*

And whaddayaknow? Sometimes three truly is a charm.

The chase ends with NutJob unrecognizable, nothing more than a pile of factory parts. The stopwatch had barely stopped before I raced, er, flippered behind NutJob, my now-accustomed-to eye shades providing no blind spots whatsoever as I easily maneuvered around the handful of undisturbed items in our path. Channeling the Kanga shepherd dog, highly regarded for its immense strength and calm courage, I summoned the brawn and backbone to finally overcome NutJob, stopping short of eating my first rodent only because I was uncertain if pug tummies can digest faux squirrels with mechanical innards.

And now I proudly float above what remains of NutJob as egghead Roger pins a blue ribbon to my wolf collar. He and the other Rogers are weeping with pride after getting a call from Administrator Jetson telling us to stand by for a congratulatory call from the President of the United States.

Er, maybe it didn't go down *exactly* like that. From the top!

The chase ends with NutJob not only unrecognizable but smashed apart, his more than three dozen pieces scattered throughout the spacecraft. All I remember is the cheers from Mission Control, and suddenly I was Rocky Pugboa in his comeback bout against NutJob

Creed. Strong uppercut! Jab to the head! Bite on the tail! Right hook! Bob and weave! Eye of the Pug!

Poor NutJob never saw me coming. I could hear Sirius the Dog Star singing "Gonna Fly Now" as I strongly and speedily flippered above, around and under the stupefied, stunned and now staggering squirrel as I pulverized him into parts. My blindered eyes may have partially obscured my vision, but nothing can obscure my vision of victory!

And now, looking around at the mess that remains of the robotic rodent, I imagine the astonished but proud faces of the four Rogers and Administrator Jetson. *Bring on the applause! Bring on the accolades! Bring on the acclaim! Bring on . . .*

I'm pulled away from my make-believe awards ceremony as that familiar high-pitched squeal sounds before the boss' voice booms in from headquarters:

"Houston to *Wolf Wanderer*! Houston to *Wolf Wanderer*!"

It takes very stunned egghead Roger a moment to weave around the squirrel's metal guts, gears and other robotic gewgaws floating about the spaceship. His head swivels from the puffed-up pug to his stupefied teammates and back to me again before taking a deep breath and then replying.

"Go ahead, Houston," he says, slapping NutJob's bushy tail out of his way.

Administrator Jetson loudly *whaps!* what sounds like a clipboard against his microphone. As he addresses us, he sounds like he's speaking through gritted teeth.

"Hmmm," he says, sarcasm lacing his tone. "Let's see. What is the first experiment called? Oh. Yes: *Pug Rodent Pursuit in Zero Gravity: Implications for Advancements in Olympic and Other Athletic Training.* Does it say 'Pug Rodent *Destruction* in Zero Gravity'? *No,* it does not."

He takes a long, clearly exasperated breath before continuing.

"Now then, certainly we cannot place the blame on PD, whose very brain is wired from birth to seek out prey and even subdue the captured quarry. I am telling you all for the second time today: the onus to clearly explain the rules of each test to PD, America's first dognaut, falls on you four.

"Get it together! The world is watching! Houston out!"

I dare a glance at the Rogers, who likely feel *thiiiiiiiiis* close to being unemployed. They avoid looking my way as they begin air-swimming around the spaceship to grab the pieces of the former devil squirrel and discard them in the box it came in.

Researcher Roger pauses in his parts-gathering and apparently decides to speak for the group.

"PD? We are sorry if we failed you. We thought we gave the instructions intelligibly, with articulation and clarity. I studied the pug manual from cover to cover to be sure we would anticipate any need for further explanation of test steps. Clearly we missed something, and I know I speak for us all when I say we can do better. We *will* do better."

I am about to acknowledge that, *Yes, of course it is your faults and not my fault!* when I notice egghead Roger checking on a control panel that our microphones are muted before nodding at his colleagues. The atmosphere turns decidedly chilly.

"PD!" Rogerette takes over as group leader. "The only thing the administrator said that I agree with was 'Get it together!' You! Not us! Don't you lose us our jobs!

"Now then! Clean up the items you somehow *again* upended, eat your dinner, and get some rest. Tomorrow's test *must* go perfectly!"

Okay, okay, I think, hanging my head and feeling chastised but forcing myself to think positively. *You all will see! No more flops, flounderings or failures! PD the dognaut will make NASA and the world proud!*

I mean, what *else* could possibly go wrong . . . ?

Experiment One

Pug Rodent Pursuit

Experiment Two
Pug Olfactory Influence on Food Choices
NASA
WW
MISSION

Chapter Five

ALL ABOARD THE VOMIT COMET

In 1957, four years before Alan Shepard became the first American in space, astronauts began training on planes that simulated weightlessness by making roller-coaster-like movements in the air. This parabolic flight path—which caused a nausea-inducing feeling of free fall—led many trainees to vomit, hence the craft's nickname: the Vomit Comet.

Sounds awful, right? Well, it's nothing compared to what I'm going through now. *Wolf Wanderer* isn't a simulation like the Vomit Comet; it's the real thing. My belly is doing loop-de-loops as I fight to hold in the tiny bit of kibble I was allowed this morning before the start of Experiment Two.

Honestly, I should be happy merely to be allowed to *do* another test, given my squirrel chase screw-up yesterday. I mean, when smiley Roger tucked me into my bedroll last night, I was worried that instead of securing me to the wall, he would toss me out of the airlock and I'd spin away like General Zod in *Superman II*, never to be seen again.

And I *was* happy. At first. When my mates woke me with the news that I'd be spending the day taste-testing, I couldn't have imagined a more fun experiment.

But then I learned *what* I'd be tasting! And that's when my queasy, qualmy tummy made me sympathize with the Vomit Comet folks and caused my round pug face to look just like that barf emoji on Mommy's iPhone.

But that came later. When I first saw what egghead Roger had written on the whiteboard, I could have leaped right over that big moon outside our spaceship. Imagine being a food-motivated pug and reading this:

Experiment Two—Pug Olfactory Influence on Ingestion Choices: Implications for Astronaut Palate Fatigue and Sustenance Sustainability on Future Multi-Year Missions

Basically, I would get to sniff and snack for hours! This looked like it was going to be the second-best day ever, the first being the day I first espied my Fawn Girl Pug Crush out on that walkie. *Eat! Eat! Eat!* And my munching actually would matter to someone other than me!

"Okay, PD, today's test is profoundly important to NASA," egghead Roger had begun as he picked up his clipboard. "It will have a huge influence on astronauts' diet and health by helping to determine what foods are served on the multi-year missions of the future.

"See, PD, astronauts have a diminished sense of taste and smell in space, which affects their appetites, and on longer missions they often experience menu fatigue. These issues can negatively impact their ability to consume adequate nutrition.

"Also, PD, future missions will require crews to be in space for years at a time. Carrying enough prepackaged food for such a voyage is neither feasible nor economically reasonable. So NASA is seeking ways to produce food items during space travel, reducing reliance on prepackaged items that would otherwise quickly be exhausted."

I had no idea what he was yammering on about. I heard, "blah blah blah Diet!" . . . "blah blah blah Appetite!" . . . "blah blah blah Consume!" . . . "blah blah blah Nutrition!" Alas, when egghead Roger is leading the lecture, the pug pupil has to be patient.

"PD, a dog's olfactory system is up to ten million times as sensitive as that of a human. So your amazing sense of smell will help you rate foods on their spiciness and flavorings and other appealing traits that will hopefully stimulate our dulled senses and encourage us astronauts to eat more."

Well, I for one am very stimulated, I had thought, wiggling about as I tried to focus on his words.

"You also are going to try some fun foods that could be created and stored easily on future lengthier expeditions in space. Plus, your superior sense of smell can provide a low-tech early warning system for chemical or spoilage problems. See?"

I do see! I thought, wagging my curly tail. *Now let's see the food!*

That's when Egghead Roger stepped away from the whiteboard, revealing the list of bizarre so-called "foods" on the taste test menu.

Lord save me, I thought. And, for the second time in as many days . . .

I hate this game.

And now here comes Rogerette, sounding like the waitress in a true Hell's kitchen.

"Just look at all the foods you get to try!" she gushes with what seems like forced enthusiasm. "There's corn smut, a mold that grows on corn! And a fermented fungus that mimics the flavor and look of octopus! And dehydrated stink bugs! And aroma pods you tuck in your cheeks to jazz up bland foods! And—oh boy, fungus burgers, PD! And 3D-printed pizza! And . . ."

My eyes blur and my stomach lurches again. *I don't wanna eat mold! I don't wanna eat octopus fungus! I don't want to eat paper from Mommy's printer!*

All I can hope at this point is that there's no robot squirrel intestines on the menu.

Just as I'm devising a plan to sneak off to the kitchen and eat some of the *real* food remaining in Kibble Bin Two, the comm system squawks to life.

"Houston to *Wolf Wanderer*, Houston to *Wolf Wanderer*," Administrator Jetson calls out.

"Go ahead, Houston," Rogerette says while simultaneously giving me a glare that warns me not to act up.

"*Wolf Wanderer*," the NASA leader begins, using a serious tone that pulls me from my Kibble Bin Two gorging fantasy. "I wanted to check in this morning before PD begins his taste-testing to remind you of the significance of this experiment. PD's findings will impact the health and possibly lives—*lives!*—of the men and women on crucial space missions, on the International Space Station, and—I cannot overstate the magnitude of this—coming expeditions to Mars and beyond. PD's decisions, judgments and verdicts regarding our space cuisine will help determine whether our crews get sufficient nourishment as they conduct the pivotal work of NASA.

"Remember, PD, NASA is counting on you. Your food findings will fuel America's continued superiority in space today, tomorrow and forever. Houston out!"

As the speaker crackles with the administrator's sign-off, I forget my revulsion about smuts and fungi and—um, octopus pizza?—and I think about the confidence Administrator Jetson has placed in me. *He just said that I, PD the PugNaut, will help develop NASA's new menu, the foods of the future aimed at keeping astronauts healthy and strong! Maybe they'll name menu items after me! PD's Pizza! PD's Peanut Butter! PD's . . .*

But as I stare at the whiteboard and the foods (??) written thereon, it occurs to me that maybe I overstated my enthusiasm about keeping astronauts hale and hearty. I mean, I want to help, but . . .

Alas, it doesn't appear that any of the Rogers will be seeking my input on the tasting menu options. I turn toward the whiteboard and see researcher Roger making notes next to the (*fake!*) foods he listed. The jottings include stuff like "Assess appetite stimulation properties" and "Note subject's ability to overcome antipathy to texture" and "Evaluate acceptance of fungus-based comestibles."

As he continues his scribbles, I find myself looking less and less forward to this test. I mean, really—why all the fretting about astronauts' wellbeing anyway? Can't they just drink Tang? You know—that orange drink powder that got all that publicity when NASA sent it on that space mission in 1962? It was good enough for John Glenn, folks.

And then I wouldn't have to eat bug smut and paper octopuses!

"Let's start with appetite stimulation, move on to novelty, and finish with sustainability and shelf stability," egghead Roger suggests to the room at large, eyes traveling to his crewmates and landing on their—suddenly appetite-less—lab rat. "PD, you should be rather ravenous given your restricted morning rations. So this should be quite pleasurable."

"Yeah, little guy," chimes in smiley Roger as he floats over to us, licking the spoon he has just dipped into a container of reconstituted freeze-dried pudding that I doubt is fungal- or bug-based. "I bet you're pitying all those dogs back on Earth who don't get to sample food all day!"

As he smacks his lips in obvious enjoyment of his tasty treat, I am overcome by a vision of my enemy Ralph leisurely lapping up his tasty kibble while I am tasked with sampling smut. I bet this whole idea was Ralph's cosmic joke on me. Wait'll I get home.

But I've no time to dream up revenge scenarios. My tummy gurgles as I watch Rogerette squeezing the last blob of peanut butter from a pouch and licking at the opening to make sure she doesn't miss one bit of this *actual* food. Then we all turn our attention back to smiley Roger, who is air-swimming toward me with what apparently is my first so-called food to try. His big arms conceal most of the item, but I think I can make out a . . . is that a *tentacle?*

I'm about to beseech what I assume is my only hope at this point—Sirius, the Dog Star—when researcher Roger clears his throat.

"PD, this one should be pretty tasty," he *lies* as he consults what I assume is some manual of cruddy cuisine. "You will be trying a mycoprotein-based alternative to octopus, made from naturally fermented mushroom mycelium. That's the part of fungus that absorbs nutrients from the environment. It's already being used for other purposes, like the creation of eco-friendly clothing and packaging."

Well, at least *something* is friendly. Certainly not Administrator Jetson or NASA or the Rogers. I thought they *liked* me. No! They are making me eat clothes and packages!

Smiley Roger, toting the fungus octopus thingy, glides over to the whiteboard and looks at the notations written next to the test items. "I think texture should be a big part of this sampling. The package insert says it's supposed to be sorta chewy, very similar to conventional octopus tentacles." Turning to me, he adds, "Maybe it'll remind you of a nice chewy bully stick, PD!"

A final prayer to the Dog Star goes unanswered as egghead Roger produces the stopwatch from yesterday's squirrel chase and says it's time to begin.

"PD," he says as I look anywhere but at smiley Roger, who's holding aloft the dreaded tentacled foodstuff, "we are going to spend thirty minutes assessing each food. You're to judge taste, texture, smell, mouthfeel, viscosity, appearance and sustainability, then rate your level of enjoyment or non-enjoyment."

I fake a big snagglegrin, feigning eagerness and enthusiasm to get going, but in reality all I want is to swim my little feet right on over to my sleep sack, zip myself in and nap until tomorrow's test which *has* to be better than this. *Please, Dog Star,* I beseech my pal Sirius, *please make it better than this.*

Smiley Roger extends a plastic forkful of the faux tentacle toward my tightly clenched jaw. I do a fierce head shake, but it's clear I'm not getting out of this. I open my mouth an inch to allow the slimy faux octopus arm in, and I . . .

Nearly gag. The slithery, icky, inky octopus leg is wiggling around my mouth as I fight my swallow reflex and then my gag reflex as the disgusting little lump of leg tries to slither its way down my esophagus. I try to evaluate "ability to stimulate appetite" and "mouthfeel and texture" and the other goals listed on the whiteboard, but the only thing I can focus on is getting this grossness out of my mouth.

Four human jaws drop as I feign a pleased look and then dog-paddle like my tail's on fire from the research room to the pantry. Before any of the Rogers can get there, I've opened the mercifully empty Kibble Bin One, spat the slimy tentacle into it, and closed the lid. And before the Rogers' surprised expressions have had the chance to change, I'm already back and giving the quartet a pleased, if faked, paws up.

"Boy, PD! You sure found that first food scrumptious, didn't you? That was quite the zippy zoomie!" smiley Roger chuckles as he tears open a packet of beef (not fungus!) jerky and pops a big piece in his mouth, causing about the loudest PD tummy growl I've ever made.

Researcher Roger holds his marker aloft as he hovers by the board. "PD really gobbled that down, gang. I am giving it a yes for palatability as well as ability to combat menu fatigue. We already know it has a long shelf life, as the properties of dried fungus have been well documented. A winner, according to PD."

The only winner is me, because I never again will have fungal tentacles in my mouth. Well, unless PD the dognaut goes to Mars. But hopefully kibble travels well and the kibble bins will be there.

Drawing me from my dogfood daydream is the arm of egghead Roger reaching past me to open a cabinet. He grabs a couple of boxes and then tries and fails to hide his disgust as he stares at the pictures on the fronts of the packages. He looks as green around the gills as Mommy did that time she found that trout behind the milk a week after she cooked it.

"Okay, PD. This next sampling should be both fun and interesting," he opines as he consults a manual whose tummy-terrorizing title is *Creepy Crawly Cuisine: The Future of Insects in Space Meal Planning* while simultaneously twirling a long strand of spaghetti around a fork and then slurping it in like he's the male lead in *Lady and the Tramp* or something.

"PD," he continues around a mouthful of mouth-watering pasta, "NASA has determined that stink bugs are highly promising as a possible protein source for future long-term missions. Stink bugs have a complete amino acid profile, which is crucial for meeting the dietary demands of astronauts. They can be ground, seasoned, and used in many dishes, and they have excellent storability."

My eyes are metaphorically swimming as rapidly as I want to air-swim away from this madness. *Stink bugs? Stink? Bugs?*

"And check it out, PD!" smiley Roger says, peering over researcher Roger's shoulder. "The potential toxins and defensive chemicals that produce their foul odor have been removed. I bet these are yum-yum-yummy!" He positively beams as he continues reading. "Says here they have an unexpected crisp apple flavor!"

Egghead Roger somehow has mastered the human art of shoving food in his mouth while interrupting another person. "Yeah," he says as he slurps in an errant noodle trying to escape his maw. "Stink bugs have many meal and snack possibilities. Baked whole, they make crunchy bug chips. Powdered stink bugs can be stirred into beverages or combined with herbs, spices and water or oil to make a delicious dip or a batter for deep-fried seafood."

Oh, thank goodness! I think. *Now I get it! It's still last night and this is just a bad dream. I am about to be gently nudged awake by researcher Roger as he announces that the real Experiment Two is called "Pug Sampling of Food in Kibble Bins Two, Three, Four and Five: Applications for Making Dogs Do Non-Stop Joy Zoomies." Yes, that has to be it because . . .*

No way am I eating Stinky McStinkBug!

Meanwhile, in the land (or space) of *real* food, egghead Roger quickly leaves and reenters the lab after evidently making a yet another visit to the kitchen, and now he is peeling apart a fat stick of string cheese that is neither stinky nor bug-based. He stares at the whiteboard while I stare at the strings of yellow goodness hanging from his mouth and hope against hope he's about to change the sampling selection. *Maybe I can rate mozzarella versus cheddar versus provolone because I love cheese and am a good judge of it and also . . .*

"PD, we have several forms of stink bug for you to try," he says, sounding like a waiter listing the day's specials. "We will start with a whole stink bug that has been prepared to have the mouthfeel of a potato chip; we will move onto a beverage resembling apple juice, made from powdered stink bug; and we'll end with a stink bug carob mousse. Wow! The folks in charge of our stink bug menu sure thought of a lot of delicious ways to enjoy stink bug!"

No they didn't! I bark inside my horrified mind. *No one can make stink bugs delicious! Not carob cultivators or flavored beverage chemists or potato chip makers! You can't improve a stinky stinkbug!*

As I continue howling in my head, Rogerette glides over to me, holding out a tray on which are three plates with domed lids. I suddenly am back in time sitting on Mommy's lap in front of the television, watching that scene in *The Green Mile* where John Coffey is getting his last meal before heading to the electric chair.

Of course *he* got to have meatloaf, mashed potatoes with gravy, okra, and Mrs. Edgecomb's cornbread. I get stink bugs.

"Mmmmm, PD!" Rogerette enthuses while looking from the tray to me and back again. "Stink bug chips and stink bug apple juice and stink bug mousse! Which do you want to try first?"

Before I can choose "none of the above," researcher Roger goes to the whiteboard and orders my bug banquet thusly:

Stink Drink—250 milliliters served in a bowl; swish contents about mouth

Stink Chips—two whole insects including shields, antennae and wings

Stink Mousse—one full 60-milliliter ramekin; PD will enjoy stink bug mashed with carob, while astronauts will have a chocolate option

"Okay, PD, let's get started," egghead Roger says, placing the bowl of apple stink drink under my nose. "Go ahead and lap it up and then give us your opinion on whether it would be enjoyable with meals on space missions."

Mimicking drinking water from my dog dish, I stick my tongue in and focus on fooling the Rogers. As I rapidly slurp up the vile liquid without actually swallowing any, my sole thought is . . .

I am not drinking Stinky, I am not drinking Stinky, I am not drinking Stinky . . .

Pretending to swallow, I give my crewmates an enthusiastic nod and then imagine their surprised stares as I bolt from the room and swim like I'm Michael Phelps to the sleep area. Fighting to keep the apple stink juice in, I go straight to researcher Roger's sleep sack and spit the beverage inside. Before the Rogers' fallen jaws are raised, I am back in the lab, looking eager to eat.

"Wow, buddy," smiley Roger laughs, "another food that really got you excited! I'm starting to envy the astronauts of tomorrow!"

The rest of the thirty minutes are torturous as my tummy revolts against the repugnant stink foods. I keep the chips and mousse in my mouth only as long as it takes me to fake the zippy zoomies to researcher Roger's bed and back. With all three stink (non)delicacies disposed of in his sleeping bag and all the Rogers thinking I'm a fan of all things stink, I sense Sirius giving PD the PugNaut a big "mission accomplished" paws up.

Now egghead Roger tells me to chill a few moments so the Rogers can grab a quick bite. I drool as smiley Roger passes around what smells like (non-bug, non-fungal-based) chicken curry wraps. Just as my (unbeknownst-to-the-crew) hollow and hungry tummy starts growling, the telltale rumble thankfully is interrupted by the crackle of the comm.

"Houston to *Wolf Wanderer*, Houston to *Wolf Wanderer* . . ."

Egghead Roger replies around a big mouthful of wrap, "Go ahead, Houston."

"Good afternoon, *Wolf Wanderer*," Administrator Jetson says, sounding upbeat. "I am assuming today's tasting is going much better than yesterday's squirrel chase.

"PD's obvious enjoyment of food coupled with his superior olfactory system makes America's first dognaut a natural for determining the menu for future space missions. His mastery in detecting and discerning odors; his appreciation of what makes truly good-tasting fare; his ability to distinguish meaty, savory, umami-rich flavors from others—these skills and more are why PD is going to be remembered forever for making our astronauts' foods nutrient-dense, flavorful, and appealing. Everyone on the NASA food science team is looking forward to his judgments regarding the samplings.

"Houston out!"

Egghead Roger signs off as he and the other Rogers finish their wraps and discuss the testing order for the rest of the foods. Meanwhile I am having a discussion as well, with myself, trying to convince future PD that the remaining samplings will be mmmm-mmmm-good and that the worst of the tastings are surely behind us.

Er . . . maybe not.

"I found the eel compost protein mix!" smiley Roger announces as he floats toward us, holding aloft a box featuring a snaky-looking creature grinning as it squats over what looks like a pile of poopie.

Researcher Roger beams as he eyes the box. "PD, this next food—should you give it an upvote—would take recycling to a new level," he begins. "You will be the first to try out what is the end result of the transformation of animal waste into edible bacteria. How exciting is that?"

"Mmmm," smiley Roger enthuses, "says here that this company created a protein powder from eel poop that tastes like cinnamon and can be sprinkled on cereal or yogurt or even used in desserts. I bet PD will be excited to try *this* one!"

I'm sorry, what?

"It's truly genius," smiley Roger cuts in. "See, PD, if successful, this will provide food for astronauts on long deep-space missions while simultaneously solving the problem of what to do with animal excrement."

I'm sorry, What?

He adds: "And the good news for you is that, according to the food scientists who created this product, the taste is sort of like a cross between chicken and fish. You'll be enjoying a sampling of what is best described as a delicious chicken- and fish-flavored smear of microbial goo."

I'm sorry, WHAT?

"And did you know eel is super high in protein? Up to 22 percent by weight!" Rogerette says, heading my way with yet another tray from Hell. "That's superb nutrition, PD!"

So are Mommy's protein shakes! I argue in my mind. *Feed the astronauts those! Not recycled eel doody!*

"Here you go, PD!" Rogerette says, holding a large serving spoon she has just filled with an eel poopie smear right under my nose. "Go ahead and give the goo a go!"

I comply, but, needless to say, the only "go" I give is a warp-speed "*go!*" from the lab to the potty area, where I quickly spit the gross gloopy goop into the toilet and then latch the lid since I don't know how the Rogers' flusher works and I can't risk poo goo floating around the spaceship. I desperately want to use the kitchen's water tank to rinse the eel poopie from my mouth, but instead I race back to the once again slack-jawed crew.

"Whoa, buddy, you're just loving all the samplings, aren't you!" smiley Roger laughs. "Yet another four paws up from our resident taster!" Looking to researcher Roger, who is at the ready with his marker by the whiteboard, he adds, "I'd give this a yes for palatability and ability to overcome the psychological aspect. Clearly PD gobbled the eel goo right down."

The rest of the day's tastings, sadly, did not get tastier. It's now nearly four o'clock and I honestly am trying to remember why I ever thought feeding time was happy time.

The poop was fittingly followed by smut. The corn-grown fungus had a not-particularly-appealing mushroomy flavor that Rogerette said was described on the accompanying pamphlet as "umami/funky—a combination of sweet, earthy, and smoky, with balsamic hints."

Well, here's a hint from PD: I hope the Rogers brought books to read, because movie night is canceled—I just spat the smut into the DVD player.

Next up was something reminiscent of cowboys in movies Mommy and I have watched where the buckaroo is chewing on a wad of chaw. This tasting had me evaluating several flavor pods that were placed between my cheek and lower jaw.

"Your superior sense of smell is really going to help us out, PD," researcher Roger had said while reading from an information packet. "You're going to try something NASA hopes will overcome our dulled sense of both smell and taste caused by the sinus congestion common in space. These edible aroma pods put concentrated scent right near the nasopharyngeal cavity to enhance the flavor of bland foods.

"So open wide and . . ."

The three flavors I was supposed to let dissipate in my little pug mouth were called yuck, yucky and yuckier. Okay, they were called chili pepper, tart lemon and anchovy paste. Following three more "happy" zoomies, each disgusting, barely dissolved pod now sits deep down in the condiment holder in the pantry.

Too bad I couldn't hide deep down in there with them.

The following fake food had the misleading name "burger." But the burgers Mommy gets at Burger 7 near our house are made of cow, not mold.

"Yum yum, PD, right?" Rogerette had said as she floated over with yet another detestable dish for me to try. She then had raised the lid to reveal a flat, gray, mushy, muddy, squishy, squidgy blecky burger wannabe. "PD, this is NASA's prototype fungus burger! It's nutritious and resource-efficient, cultivated as a mycoprotein biomass and created entirely in a bioreactor!"

This confusing, confounding news was followed by a five-minute standoff during which egghead Roger and researcher Roger tried to pry open my clamped chompers while Rogerette held the mold meat an inch from my maw.

I did lose that battle. But Rogerette will learn she is the bigger loser, because moments after the Rogers forced the gray gunk into my mouth, I did my zealous zoomie right to her cosmetics case and swapped out her creams for burger blech.

Enjoy that mud mask.

The final stop on my tour of Hades was an ersatz pizzeria.

"PD, imagine enjoying a slice of home while on Mars!" smiley Roger had said as he carried over a large plate holding a deceptively real-looking piece of pepperoni pizza.

But as I drooled over the idea of eating something actually delicious after all the yuck I'd had in my mouth today, researcher Roger just had to ruin the pizza party. Drifting over with a manual titled *NASA Foods of Future Missions*, he cleared his throat and spent the next several minutes spoiling my appetite.

"PD," he began, looking down at the book, "spaceflight foods of tomorrow will rely heavily on 3-D printing. And *you* get to sample one of the first prototypes. NASA has companies working to build food using 3-D printers—food just like the scrumptious-looking pizza you're about to enjoy."

Huh? Paper pizza?

"Yeah, just think, PD!" smiley Roger interjected with more delight than digital pizza warranted as he looked over his crewmate's shoulder at the manual. "Every bit of this yummy slice of pizza was created layer by layer on a 3-D printer! Everything from the crust to the sauce to the pepperoni to the veggies was deposited from cartridges containing powdered carbohydrates, veggies, proteins, fats, and oils."

The only good part of this deceptive deep-dish was the absence of mushroom topping. I guess NASA figured I'd had my fill of fungus today.

"Your assessment is crucial here, PD," researcher Roger stressed as he looked from me to the pretend pizza. "NASA is again relying on your outstanding sense of smell, this time to see if precise positioning of aroma compounds can improve taste perception and trigger appetite regulating centers in the brain."

There was more technobabble—stuff about how technology would add micronutrients, flavor, the aforementioned aroma and more to all the coming comestibles astronauts would get from printer trays. And about the importance of aroma in encouraging astronauts to eat more and not get malnourished.

But I'd long since zoned out and was focused solely on a *way* out.

Unfortunately, it appeared the only way out was temporarily letting the paper pizza in. So I did a snagglegrin as phony as the food before me and reluctantly opened my mouth and . . .

My final "Wow, I love this fake food!" zippy zoom was a pizza delivery to the den. I hurried to the box of old-timey board games, then spit out the slice, tore it into pieces, and put some in Candy Land, some in Yahtzee, some in Clue, and the rest in the aptly named Aggravation.

It's now nearly six p.m. As I hurry back to the lab after hiding the last of the day's inedible edibles, I make it to the table just as the speaker again squawks to life.

"Houston to *Wolf Wanderer*, Houston to *Wolf Wanderer.*"

"Go ahead, Houston," Rogerette says.

"How are things going with the last of PD's tastings, *Wolf Wanderer*?" Administrator Jetson inquires. "I assume PD has made it through all the foods by now."

"Great timing, Houston," says Rogerette, giving me an approving look. Her expression is one I haven't seen from her since the lecture over my threatening the Rogers' jobs. "PD just finished enjoying his pepperoni pizza, and we are simply *thrilled* to say he clearly loved every single item! Based on his enthusiastic reactions, we gave all tested items high marks for all categories."

"Great to hear!" Administrator Jetson exclaims, his rich voice reverberating around the spacecraft. "PD's work will have a huge impact on the space menu of tomorrow. His keen sense of smell paired with his superior ability to assess appealing food will forever free astronauts from palate fatigue and resultant malnutrition and other health problems. Nice work, PD!

"Now go reward our star taster with extra kibble! And the rest of you enjoy your dinner! Too bad there was only one slice of that delicious 3-D pizza! Houston out!"

Following the sign-off, it's head pats all the way around for dognaut PD: NASA's protector of the palate! NASA's master of menu monotony! NASA's disciple of deliciousness!

And now it's nine p.m. and the five of us are happily satiated, having had our bellies filled with non-bug, non-fungal, non-paper food. As I am tucked into my sleeping bag by egghead Roger, I grin thinking about how I fooled everyone and how I have helped NASA solve the problem of astronaut palatability and malnutrition without actually swallowing one morsel featured on the tasting menu.

Well, I think as I drift off, *at least until the Rogers decide to watch a movie, or play a board game or peer into Kibble Bin One, or do a mud mask. But otherwise, dognaut PD will forever be recognized as the dog whose sense of smell saved NASA's future astronauts from ill health.* My snagglegrin is as bright as the big moon outside as I nod off and dream of my Fawn Girl Pug Crush and me dancing amongst the stars and . . .

Moments later I bolt awake as a loud, angry cry thunders from the bed of researcher Roger.

"What is this gloppy muck in my bed?!!"

Oh no! Save me, Sirius!

KIBBLE
BIN
ONE
CANDYLAND
AGGRAVATION
NASA
WW MISSION

Experimen three
Walkies in zero gravity to reduce obesity
NASA
WW
SSION
5kg
5kg
W W
MI SSION
TIME :00:0 LEVEL:00
SPEED:0km/hr
STOP
NASA
WW
MISS

Chapter Six

IF A BLACK PUG FALLS INTO A BLACK HOLE . . .

In April 2007, astronaut Sunita Williams virtually joined the more than 20,000 people participating in the Boston Marathon as she ran a marathon in space. Using a treadmill aboard the International Space Station, Williams completed her 26.2-mile run in four hours and twenty-four minutes.

While it might be rare for an astronaut to run a marathon, long workouts in space actually are the norm. In order to prevent the loss of muscle and bone caused by being in microgravity, the Rogers and all astronauts perform an average of two and a half hours of combined cosmic cardio and stellar strength training every day they are in space.

Luckily for me, I thus far have been allowed to just hover amongst their floating sweat droplets while the Rogers do acrobics and pump iron after tethering and hooking and looping themselves onto the treadmill or the bikes or the machines that simulate weightlifting. I thank Sirius and my other lucky stars that the Rogers have until now excused me from gym class; I guess they figure I have been getting plenty of exercise chasing robot squirrels and getting countless attacks of the zoomies.

Alas, time to lace up the trainers. Smiley Roger woke me this morning with the news that the third and final experiment will involve my going on some walkies! While the word *walkie* generally is music to my button ears, I'm not sure I trust that these walkies are going to be like the happy ones I go on with Mommy. Considering what I've endured the past two days, I fear this third experiment will prove the old saw that bad things come in threes.

This rousing by smiley Roger actually was my second wakening since being secured in my sleep sack last night. I had just nodded off and was enjoying a delightful dream about finally pugging up and approaching my Fawn Girl Pug Crush and then planning our wedding and our happily-ever-after when a howl scarier than I've heard in my seven-year-long life roared through the sleep section of the spacecraft.

"What is this gloppy muck in my bed?!!"

The bellowing from researcher Roger replaced the bellowing bullmastiff barking at my beloved and me in my dream. I opened my eyes to find myself back in the spaceship . . . and desperately wishing I were still in dreamland.

"I want to know who put this gross, gunky yuck in my sleeping bag!" The moonlight outside *Wolf Wanderer*'s window had illuminated the whites of researcher Roger's glaring eyes as they traveled the room before alighting on me. "PD? Did *you* spit this into my bed? Is this one of the foods from your *experiment*?"

I had momentarily considered staging a defense, explaining that, no, in fact, I did not spit food into his bed since certainly nothing I sampled that day could be considered food. But given his anger as he air-paddled to a cabinet for a towel and a clean sleep sack, I thought showing him my level ten snagglesmile might be a better way to earn his forgiveness.

Sadly, his shriek was just the first of many as one after the next hidey-hole was discovered. While researcher Roger was finding himself in a bed of slimy stink bug, Rogerette was doing her pre-bed beauty ritual, applying what she assumed was face cream. Well, if she didn't want fungus burger face, she shouldn't have forced it in a certain dognaut's mouth.

The next fun find was by egghead Roger, who was visiting the little boys' room before settling down for the night. Since I had tossed the masticated eel compost in the loo without actually sitting on the potty seat, the pressure switch that controls the fan-driven suction system didn't activate. Poor egghead Roger. With no gravity to keep the spit up eel poopie in the bowl, he was greeted with a face full of eel poo and angrily spent the next twenty minutes corralling the floating foulness into several baggies.

You'd think all that would be more than enough yelling for one evening, but smiley Roger announced about an hour later that he couldn't sleep and was going to go watch a movie. Which was not an option, of course, due to the corn smut in the DVD slot. And his idea of playing a solo game of Candy Land didn't go well, either; and finding the spit-up pizza made him curious enough to check the other board games. So no entertainment for him. Or anyone else until the DVD player and the games are cleaned and disinfected.

So, once again, I am starting the day not on any of the Rogers' good lists.

Somehow, despite my waning popularity, I haven't been voted off the spaceship. I suspect this is mostly because they need me for today's third and—mercifully—final experiment of the *Wolf Wanderer* mission. I did get a long lecture from the Rogers, who took turns dressing me down for having botched both the mutant squirrel chase and the mutant food tasting.

But after venting, the Rogers seem happy with me again. And now smiley Roger is taking me out of my bedroll and explaining the day's test as we head to the kitchen for breakfast.

"This is one you will love, little buddy!" he enthuses as I stare at him skeptically. "You get to spend the day doing something you doggies truly enjoy while making enormously impactful contributions to science! What do you think of *that*, PD?"

What I think is that the Rogers are Lucy holding the football in those *Charlie Brown* comics and I am chump Charlie about to be foiled again.

As I hover over the dining table, watching Rogerette approach with my kibble, I note egghead Roger simultaneously emerging from the pantry with a frown on his face. *Uh oh,* I think as his squinty eyes find my googly ones and I see that one hand is holding his coffee cup and the other is holding the condiment container.

The condiment container that has salt, pepper, sugar, spices . . . and PD-saliva-coated aroma pods.

"PD?" His eyes narrow even further. "Why is there a sucked-on, wet aroma pod in the Coffee-mate? And why do I think I will find pieces of soggy, moist aroma pods in every item in this container?"

I feign innocence, square my withers, and pose as the very paragon of virtue. I feel my chubby cheeks straining with effort as I beam a wide grin, which sadly has no effect on egghead Roger who stink-eyes me with every sip of his creamer-less coffee.

Coming to my rescue is researcher Roger, who pushes back from his plate of reconstituted powdered eggs and announces it's time to get started on the day's tests. He hustles to the research room to retrieve another one of his heavy tomes before gliding over to me and reaching for my leash with his free hand. I gobble down the last two pieces of kibble in my bowl and lick a crumb from my upper lip, pondering whether I have sufficient calories in my pug belly to power me through today's trial.

We all air-swim to the little *Wolf Wanderer* gym, where researcher Roger has set up the whiteboard. The rest of us float above the workout equipment while he pulls his dry-erase marker from his pocket; everyone's attention is drawn to the squeak of the marker as he writes the title of today's trial on the board:

Experiment Three: Pug Walks in Zero Gravity: Impacts on Canine Exercise Motivation and Reduction of Canine Obesity and Associated Poor Health

Even though happy Roger told me my third trial involves taking some walkies, actually seeing it in writing forces me to restrain the inner zoomie that wants to zip and whip and whirl and twirl all over the spaceship. *This is a test that I will pass with flying colors! No mutant monster rodents trying to kill me! No inedible fungus shoved in my mouth! Walkies! Glorious walkies!*

Snapping me out of my daydream of holding paws with my pal Sirius as we stroll through the Milky Way, gaily gallivanting around our galaxy, is a loud "Ahem" from researcher Roger who has opened the manual he brought with him earlier. On its cover is a portly pooch sitting next to a dog dish overflowing with kibble.

"PD," he begins as he looks at me over the top of the textbook, "today's experiment is profoundly important to every dog that is obese, physically challenged, injured or otherwise unable to easily exercise. The goal of this trial is to assess how weightlessness affects how a dog exercises. The hope is that our findings will lead to a reduction in obesity and associated joint pain and chronic health conditions in overweight and senior dogs."

Consulting his manual, he continues. "PD, nearly sixty percent of dogs in North America are overweight or obese. Many physical challenges facing dogs today are the result of their overweight status—conditions like arthritis, hip dysplasia, luxated patellae, general joint pain and more. These conditions reduce a dog's mobility and willingness to engage in exercise.

"NASA has tasked us with determining whether walking in zero gravity—while being *rewarded* for increasing the pace while doing so—would make exercise both easier and more enjoyable for these dogs.

"Just think, PD," concludes researcher Roger as he stares into my wide eyes. "Your walks here today could lead to innovations that bring about the end of dog chubbiness and related challenges."

As I consider the importance of my stroll, I suddenly hear a loud *Grrrrr* and am so scared that I strain against my leash.

"Wow, PD! Your belly sure is rumbling! I heard it clear from the pantry!" Rogerette laughs as she comes back into the workout area carrying four pouches of Strawberry Cheesecake Dippin' Dots, which she doles out to everyone but me. Noting my pout, she explains, "PD, I'm afraid you're not allowed snackies now; you can't be digesting lots of food while trotting on the treadmill. Sorry, but those are the orders from headquarters!"

Speaking of which, moments later, Administrator Jetson's booming baritone causes five heads to snap to attention.

"Houston to *Wolf Wanderer*, Houston to *Wolf Wanderer*." The boss' voice holds that tone he tends to use when he is about to deliver critical news.

"Go ahead, Houston," egghead Roger says. "We all are standing by in the *Wolf Wanderer* gymnasium."

I hear a long, loud intake of breath and prepare for an inspirational speech aimed at driving home the momentousness of something that until now I've considered a fun but ultimately inconsequential activity.

"PD, the problem of canine obesity is, shall we say, a *weighty* matter. Today's treadmill trials, if successful, will mean better health for your dog brethren for generations to come. While you might deem these walks to be no more taxing than your daily constitutional, the prominence of these promenades cannot be overstated.

"PD, I join all of NASA in beaming with pride at the mere thought of the leaps and bounds that *your* leaps and bounds today will bring to the science of animal health. You, PD, could literally *walk* science toward implements and innovations that lead to better lives for dogs! We are counting on you, PD! Get on that treadmill and make us proud! Houston out!"

The squeal from the microphone as Administrator Jetson signs off is reminiscent of the squeak from Dog, my most treasured toy in my bed back home. I fight homesickness as I consider how a traipse on a treadmill could improve dog lives. I guess that makes me a little less sad about not getting any Dippin' Dots.

"Okay, time for our dog to slog!" researcher Roger announces as he coasts over to the trash compactor and deposits the human crew's empty Dippin' Dots pouches inside. He then sails to the whiteboard and withdraws the dry-erase marker from his shirt pocket while egghead Roger takes my leash and leads me over to the treadmill, where his other two colleagues are waiting.

Moments later, egghead Roger and Rogerette have fitted me into a NASA-designed four-point harness sporting tiny cartoon icons of a white wolf running against a backdrop of silver stars. My harness then is tethered to the treadmill via a strong bungee cord.

As egghead Roger latches the last of the straps to the treadmill, smiley Roger approaches holding what sorta looks like a mini ball launcher like baseball players use for batting practice. I watch with curiosity as he attaches it to a bracket above the treadmill's control panel so that it faces the belt. He then pulls a remote from his shirt pocket and hits a button that causes a mechanical arm in the launcher to *whirrr!* to life and then *snap!* forward like it's the arm of baseball great Cy Young or something. "Okay, PD, ready to get some cardio and save some dog lives?" Egghead Roger's voice pulls my hypnotized focus from watching the launcher's arm fly forward over and over and over. I look to the whiteboard where he is standing alongside researcher Roger, the latter holding his dry-erase marker aloft as he prepares to write.

He turns to the board, and under:

Pug Walks in Zero Gravity: Impacts on Canine Exercise Motivation and Reduction of Canine Obesity and Associated Poor Health

he puts:

PD Treadmill Test Goals:

and writes a fat *1, 2* and *3*.

While he scribbles something next to each number, Rogerette comes our way with another box, this one bearing a picture of a merry mutt dancing with a Milk-Bone Mini that looks just like the ones Mommy gives me. As she opens the box and dumps its contents into the launching machine, I suddenly am extremely enthusiastic to exercise.

Saliva floats over my happy head as egghead Roger turns from me to the whiteboard and reads over his colleague's shoulder. I can hear them quietly yet animatedly talking, but I am too anxious to get to the Milk-Bone part of the test to care much about what they are saying. Until . . .

". . . because too many treats contradicts goal number one, which is, as you wrote, *Treadmill Walking and Weight Loss.* Loss! As in, not gaining more weight!" egghead Roger spits.

"But your argument is rendered moot by goal number two, which is *Low-Calorie Rewards to Encourage Movement.* Low-calorie! Movement!" researcher Roger hisses back.

"No! Because the third and final goal of the test is *Accelerated Ambulation for Accelerated Treat Allotment.* We must consider that although the fat or physically challenged canine is burning more calories by moving faster, his calorie burn could be *negated* by the extra food!"

"Guys! Stop already!" Rogerette snaps. "These Milk-Bone Minis are only five calories per treat! So while, *yes*, they are caloric, PD running here in zero gravity and other dogs racing about in simulated weightlessness on Earth certainly burn more calories than they are taking in!"

Smiley Roger gives me a pat as he jumps in. "Exactly! And all the while, dogs will be losing weight thanks to being rewarded *only* when exercising with as much vigor as their individual health status allows. So their treat intake is limited if they don't exercise as hard as possible!"

Wait. What? I swivel my confused head from one Roger to the next. *Rewarded only when exercising? Treat intake limited? Running?!?*

As I try and fail to keep beaming the smile that lit up my face when I first saw the Milk-Bone Mini box, reality rains on my previously sunny self. While the experiments I am doing here on *Wolf Wanderer* are aimed at leading scientists to invent great stuff, there sure hasn't been anything great for poor PD. And I think, for the third time in as many days . . .

I hate this game.

"All right, PD, let's rev up the treadmill, shall we?" researcher Roger says as he doublechecks that I'm securely tethered to the machine. "We will start with a slow walk, then go a bit faster, and then introduce rewards that will be tied to your picking up the pace, okay?"

As I fight to hide my panic as I consider what "a bit faster" might mean, egghead Roger reaches over to turn the treadmill on and I see TIME, SPEED, LEVEL and PAUSE all light up in red letters. The ON button flashes; to its right are OFF and—thank you, Sirius!—a large EMERGENCY STOP button.

"PD, this is important," says egghead Roger, and I tamp down my anxiety and try to focus on his words. "The treadmill has ten speed levels and is equipped with pace-sensing technology. As you *walk* and then *jog* and, finally, *run* to earn those tasty treats, the level will automatically adjust upward."

I look from him to the panel. *How upward are we talking?* I wonder. I need a nappie just hearing the assignment.

"The goal is to reach level 10 and . . ."

Oh. Apparently very upward.

". . . faster cadence means faster treat disbursement. Once your pace hits level 5, you will be running rather than trotting, and the mechanical arm will begin tossing treats at the rate of five per minute, or one every twelve seconds. Slowing down will stop the arm. Every minute, the level will increase, and if you can match the treadmill's speed, you will accordingly earn more treats per minute until you hit level 10."

As the room fades in and out, I try and psych my noggin into believing I am the canine reincarnation of Jesse Owens. But my noggin has checked out. My vision is going dark like the emptiest cosmic void; I feel my heart pounding in my chest and sense a *thrum! thrum! thrum!* in my little ears.

"All right, PD," says researcher Roger. "In thirty seconds, you are going to feel some air under your belly"—here I look down and see rows of tiny holes on the treadmill belt—"and then the belt will slowly start moving and you will begin walking.

"The treadmill generates an upward flow of air that forms a cushion under you. You will sort of levitate over the belt, your paws making just enough contact for you to maintain balance. The air cushion lessens your weight on the walking surface and reduces impact on your joints."

Levitate? My snaggletooth gleams as I stare at him, hopefully appearing engrossed in his words, but really my mind is back on Earth, where I am . . .

The Amazing Flying PD! Soaring over the walkie paths! Peeing on Ralph the Dog's head as I Glide! Then Swoop! And Pee! I coast over the neighborhood, using my newfound aerial acrobatic talents to easily seek out my Fawn Girl Pug Crush and then lift her into my loving forelimbs and . . .

"Three! Two! One! Machine on!" Rogerette hollers. My vision of flying with my pug love vanishes, and suddenly I am back on the treadmill, being propelled both forward a tiny bit upward as the belt begins going 'round and 'round and a cool, strange-feeling force of air hits my barrel belly. Risking a glance at the panel, I am relieved to see it says LEVEL 1. *This is a snap!* I think. *Slower than a walkie with Mommy, even!*

"PD, in sixty seconds, you are going to start increasing your speed," egghead Roger announces from his position over the machine's control panels. "When you reach level 5, we will turn on the treat dispenser."

As I march slowly on, the air current causes my stout self to alternate between hovering just above the belt to lightly touching it with my paws. It's sorta like doing a walkie on tippy-paws. I find myself enjoying the ramble, but I'm also hyperaware that, in about ten more seconds . . .

"And . . . Speed up!" Rogerette shouts as egghead Roger monitors the display. As I walk faster, I glance over to see a bright red LEVEL 2 now on the panel. Before I know it, two minutes have passed, two more commands to "Move it!" have been issued, and my now-quadrupled pace demands all my focus on what is now a semi-levitated jog.

"Sixty seconds until running speed, PD!" Rogerette announces. "And then we will start the treat machine! Remember: more movement, more Minis!"

The minute passes in what seems mere seconds. As smiley Roger offers what he assumes is an encouraging two thumbs up, I beseech Sirius for stamina. And, seconds later . . .

I'm galloping like Secretariat breaking all Triple Crown records. Except I don't possess Big Red's physicality, and while I'm sure his alleged twenty-two-pound heart could easily have handled this run, my little pug heart is slamming against my ribs as I prepare to go home to Heaven and meet God and . . . we are only at level 5!

"Treats on!" Rogerette commands, and smiley Roger hits the lever that brings the mechanical arm to life. "Run, PD! Faster, PD! No slowing down! Or no treats for you!" she screams at me.

My paws touch and hover, touch and hover, touch and hover. My heart is begging me to just give up and lie down when suddenly . . .

Thwack! The first Milk-Bone Mini is hurled toward me. Unfortunately I am not in baby-bird-mouth-wide-open mode, and so it simply sails over my head and off toward the *Wolf Wanderer* ceiling. As a food-motivated pug, missing my first morsel causes me to tap an energy reserve I didn't know I possess. *Move it!* I coach myself. *Don't slow down! Don't stop the treats!*

And about five seconds later:

Thwack! A treat whaps my nose . . .

Thwack! Slaps my head beside my left ear . . .

Thwack! Smacks my mid-sternum . . .

Thwack! Thwack! Thwack!

Ignoring the crying protests from my treat-pummeled body, I channel Cincinnati Reds great Johnny Bench, the famed catcher whose huge right hand was photographed holding seven baseballs. *I'm like the leader of the Big Red Machine!* I think as I keep up my now-level-7 pace on the treadmill belt and imagine the roar from the crowd at Riverfront Stadium as I open my mouth for the Milk-Bone Mini hurled toward me by the automatic arm.

Caught! The crowd goes wild! I'm lifted aloft by my teammates as Mommy, back home watching me on TV, bawls happy tears and . . .

"PD! You've slowed to level 2!" egghead Roger yells irritably from his spot at the machine's console. "You've caused the treat dispenser to stop until you are back at level 5! And that's only halfway to level 10, which you must attain to successfully complete the experiment!

"Now move your furry rump!"

My desire to get more Milk-Bone Minis and, okay, I guess also to help obese and physically challenged dogs overrides my innate proclivity to come to a full stop and take a nap on the treadmill belt. I hustle my way back up to level 5 and am happy to see the mechanical arm come back to life. I fight to keep my harnessed self in the center of the belt as my mind sings *Milk-Bone Mi-ni! Milk-Bone Mi-ni! Milk-Bone Mi-ni!* in time with my paw-falls.

But no Minis are coming. The arm is rotating. But . . . where are the Minis?

My heart pounds as I work to keep up with the continually increasing pace. And as I get more and more winded, it occurs to me that the belt speed has been accelerating faster than I remember. I glance toward the console and am a wee bit unsettled by the mischievous grin I spy on egghead Roger's face as he winks at smiley Roger, who still is manning the treat tossing device. Which, despite my racing along, is not rewarding my efforts.

"Here's the deal, PD," begins researcher Roger, who has left the whiteboard and now hovers over me, hands on hips, furrowed brow, tightened jaw. "We all conferred while you were getting thumped by the treats. And we have decided that in order for obese dogs to slim down, they really need to 'burn to earn.' I mean, too many treats for fat dogs during walks would sorta defeat the purpose, right?"

Wait! What? I stare at him incredulously. *How are we discussing "too many" treats? I thus far have had precisely one treat!*

Ignoring the confused look on my face, researcher Roger turns and nods to Rogerette, who floats over and takes his place. I am fighting a freakout as I see the console hit LEVEL 8 and feel the blood pulsing in my little ears—*whoosh! whoosh! whoosh!*—as I try to concentrate on her words while not passing out.

"PD! We told you to keep up the pace!" she barks. "We now think that you will be more motivated to attain level 10 if reward delivery starts at level 9, 'k?"

No, not "'k"! Definitely not "'k"! I fume inwardly as my sore paw pads alternate between hitting and hovering. My heart is ticking like a manic metronome as I race along while staring at the rotating-but-empty mechanical arm. I'm puffing in body while huffing in mind over the Rogers' arbitrary rule change.

The next thing I know, what feels like ten full minutes at level 9 have passed and my heart is pounding so hard I'm praying there's one of those automated external defibrillators on this ship. Just as I am expecting to hear "Begin chest compressions! Shock advised! Clear!" and other stuff I've heard on *ER* reruns . . .

Thwack!

Even though that treat bonked my butt, even though I am running so hard I am certain I am flying faster than *Wolf Wanderer* itself, I imagine my ink-black pupils in full dilation as I fix my focus on that mechanical arm. I open my jaw wider than its hinges should allow and lock my eyes on the treat tosser as it hurls the next Mini and . . .

"Move it PD! Faster, PD! Hit level 10, PD! Shake a leg, PD!" Rogerette roars, causing a startled me to stumble on the belt as yet another Mini sails past. Thankfully my harness is well-secured to the machine via the bungee cord, so I don't fly clear off.

Egghead Roger hits the emergency stop button while Rogerette gives me a disappointed lecture while re-securing the cords and straps.

"PD, listen up!" she says after making sure I again am in the center of the belt. "Administrator Jetson was very clear that the very *lives* of unhealthy and disabled dogs are in your little paws. Now stop messing around and hit level 10! And stop missing rewards!"

Does she think a pug *would* try *to miss catching tiny crunchy munchy yummy dog bone treats?* I grumble to myself. *I mean, they underfed me at breakfast time so I'd be hungry and then denied me a Dippin' Dots so why would . . .*

"Get ready and . . . GO!" screams Rogerette as researcher Roger twirls his marker-holding hand in that "get moving" gesture Mommy does when I'm sniffing a poopie too long on a walkie and egghead Roger stretches his mouth into a Grinch pseudogrin as he gleefully gawks at the console.

Whoa! Whoa Whoa Whoa! The belt has gone from zero to zipping as level 5 somehow becomes my starting point. The air under my belly alleviates a bit of the stress on my bustling body, but golly, not much. *I'm not warmed up! I'm not ready!*

As if reading my mind, smiley Roger smiles at me from behind the mechanical arm and attempts to put his usual positive spin on things.

"PD, guess what? We are starting you at level 5 so you can get a treat sooner! Isn't that fantastic?"

I don't know what he thinks "fantastic" means, I grouse inwardly. *What I do know is these rule-bending cheating cheaters aren't giving me any Minis until I hit level 9, which . . .*

"Hustle it up, slowpoke!" egghead Roger yips at me from the console. "Every ten seconds, I want you up another level! Hit level 6! *Now!*"

Thirty seconds later my bouncing self is semi-levitating at level 9. Half an inch above the belt, back down, back up, bounce, bounce, bounce. In my mind's eye I'm the sole pug in the English Greyhound Derby, wowing the fans at Towcester Greyhound Stadium as I whizz past the skinny entrants on my way to winning the silver trophy, the name *PD* etched on the prestigious award.

Or maybe not.

Whoa! Wait! Too much! Too fast! Another ten seconds have zipped by and I'm now flying down the belt at level 10, willing my body to fight off the complete exhaustion trying to overtake me. Tiny spheres of drool float from my panting maw toward the gym ceiling as I metamorphose from greyhound to tumbleweed, a bouncing bundle of pug stumbling and staggering along the speeding machine; I'm ping-ponging all over the belt as I tangle myself up in my tether.

I try but fail to regain my footing as my sweaty paw pads slip off the sides of the flying treadmill; only the bungee cord is keeping me centered on the belt. As the lactic acid builds up in my flagging, aching muscles, I'm about to give up when . . .

Thwack!

As a Mini flies overhead, I look up from the racing belt to see the smiling face of smiley Roger, who has just reactivated the treat-pitching arm. I summon my last reserve of energy, swallow the building saliva to clear my mouth for Minis, and . . .

Thwack! Caught!

Thwack! Caught!

Thwack! Caught!

Just as I'm starting to gain a bit of confidence, egghead Roger unexpectedly hits the emergency stop, triggering a sudden deceleration from level 10 to zero and causing this dining-and-dashing dog to ricochet from the treadmill to the whiteboard to the table holding the Milk-Bone container and back again as the bungee cord strains against its anchoring hook. My heart is still pounding from the past ten minutes of exertion as I finally come to a stop in the middle of the belt, my mind still catching up to the fact that the treat part of this game apparently has ended.

"Okay, PD, researcher Roger calls as he repositions the knocked-over whiteboard, "not too bad on the treat catching; you *did* show that a dog will exercise for food and *also* that running while periodically floating above the treadmill belt relieves stress on a dog's joints.

"Since you did such an adequate job, we are going to let you perform Treadmill Test Two, which NASA told us to administer in the event you didn't botch up the treat part of the test like you've botched up everything else."

He pauses as smiley Roger unhelpfully yells out, "Nice going, little buddy! Way to not totally blow another experiment!"

Researcher Roger taps the whiteboard to recapture my attention, and I see that he has written *Treadmill Test Two: Toy Motivation.* I really like toys! So despite feeling knackered at the very idea of even a level 1 walkie, I suddenly experience a surge of vim and vigor.

Eager for the toy trial, I note Rogerette approaching smiley Roger with another box; the latter is dismantling the treat launching machine as the former starts unpacking her parcel. From my spot on the treadmill I can't see what's in it but find myself hoping it's lots of toys.

"PD," researcher Roger says, "since you've shown that a dog is motivated to move if it is rewarded with treats, let's see if it's motivated to do so if rewarded with play." He continues with an impish grin: "And guess what? This part of the experiment involves a reunion with a great love of yours."

I giddily whip my head around looking for Dog, my favorite toy. Or Mommy! Or maybe my pal Rory Rottweiler from my fifth book, *Furry Fairy Tails.* I sing excitedly to myself, *Who's here? Who's here? Who's here?* as I simultaneously note that Rogerette has reached into the box she brought in and . . .

No! No no no! My heart hammers twice as hard as it did at level 10 as I see Rogerette holding what might as well be the devil himself here to poke my rump with his pitchfork as I run.

Although it's a furry toy and not a factory-made robot, my NASA frenemies have somehow found a toy squirrel that looks eerily, creepily, uncannily similar to NutJob. *A resurrected NutJob!* I panic as I cower. *Same scary eyes! Same pointy teeth! NutJob back from the grave!*

I hear loud crying and look around before realizing it's me. I've keeled over onto the belt—perfectly still, mouth agape and drooling like I'm playing possum.

Smiley Roger floats over and picks me up to the extent my tether allows. "What's wrong, little buddy? It's a toy for you to chase! I know you love toys and squirrels! This is going to be so fun!"

He rubs my head with a laugh and heads back to the area over the console. He holds out his hand for Rogerette to give him the—*Satan!*—squirrel and begins attaching it to a couple of taut wires and then to a rod that is affixed to the console. Then egghead Roger pulls a remote control from that box and starts making the—*Son of NutJob!*—squirrel wiggle and twitch and spin.

"PD! You can do this," Rogerette gushes, trying to calm me. "It's a darling little squirrel toy that you get to chase. Pretend you are out with your Mommy and you see a squirrel and pretend you get loose of your leash! Fun!"

Then her expression goes from saccharin-sweet to lemon-sour. "Now get it together and stop acting up!"

Moments later, I've been repositioned in the center of the treadmill, harness checked, bungee cord checked, pulse checked, sanity checked. I pug up and take another look at the alleged toy. And, okay, *maybe* this one has normal brown plastic toy eyes, and *maybe* it doesn't have teeth, and *maybe* it isn't holding a pitchfork.

But I still don't trust it.

"PD, it's nearing dinnertime, so we will try and wrap up the toy reward test within the hour. I bet you're getting hungry!" researcher Roger says from the whiteboard where he annoyingly is scarfing Dippin' Dots from a pouch in one hand as he holds his marker with his other hand to record my actions.

"We will zip through the early levels to get you warmed up. When you hit level 5, the squirrel will begin moving about. The faster you run, the closer the toy will come toward you; and if you hit level 10, the toy will be at eye level and you will get a chance to catch your first-ever squirrel in your mouth!"

I'm more annoyed that he (correctly) assumes I've never caught a squirrel than I am over being denied a bite of the Dippin' Dots. But no time to grouse, because . . .

"Three! Two! One! Go, PD!" screeches Rogerette. As I begin walking and LEVEL 1 flashes on the console, the now-familiar air begins puffing, again pushing me slightly upward and then letting my paws touch the belt, over and over.

My weary limbs reach level 5 so quickly that I'm unprepared for the loud *Kuk! Kuk! Kuk! Screech! Chirp!* that immediately brings to mind the nightmare chase of two days prior. As that demon rodent comes alive and wiggles around teasingly above and beyond my racing reach, I relive the trauma and my body unsuccessfully tries to both run and cower. Only the tethered harness prevents me from soaring up, up and away to my beloved sleep sack.

As I jet along, I spy egghead Roger using the remote to marionette the wires controlling the worst toy I've ever been told to play with; seconds later, the squirrel's plushy, plucky little legs are scissoring my way in an eerie lurching lope and its fluffy tail is swishing and flicking in a fiendish taunt.

As I remember researcher Roger's utterance of the word *dinnertime*, I suddenly want revenge. This toy *is* dinnertime! This *Wolf Wanderer* wolfdog is going to wolf down NutJob Two!

"PD! Your slobbery drool drops are floating in my face!" Rogerette kvetches as she soaks up a sweat globule with her Dippin' Dots napkin. "You've been at level 5 for nearly two minutes and you're staring and glaring at the poor little toy like a deranged nut! Now get to level 6 immediately!"

Hearing the word *nut* invokes such fear that I'm easily able to reach levels 6, 7 and even 8 within sixty seconds, due to the ancestral fight-or-flight response awakened within. My brain screams *Flee NutJob! Flee NutJob! Flee NutJob!* in tempo with my fleet feet as I am forced to chase the very monster I want to escape.

As my speed increases, Son of NutJob bobs closer to my head. I feign courage and tell myself this is my chance. I can get even! *Dinnertime! Dinnertime! Dinnertime!* I sing to myself, staring at the toy that represents the reincarnation of my biggest-ever bully.

I hear an unexpected "Whoop!" from generally unemotional egghead Roger as—within another minute—I reach level 10. NutJob-but-not-NutJob suddenly looms large, just above eye level, and I realize this is it—the moment of reckoning, NutJob's Judgment Day. I perfectly time the opening of my mouth with the puff of air propelling my stout self off the belt and . . .

Chomp!

The roar I imagine from the cheering crowd at sold-out Riverfront Stadium is a mere whisper compared to the deafening, thunderous, earsplitting roar from my crewmates. It takes a moment for their words to hit; I'm much too busy doing my victory lap, both running and dancing on the belt as I hold firmly to the treacherous toy, waving it around like a batter rounding the bases. It's all I can do to not extend a forepaw toward the heavens in victory like I'm Barry Bonds after hitting career home run number 756.

"PD! What have you done?" egghead Roger snaps as he abruptly hits the stop button, causing me to fly hither and thither, appearing to all onlookers like a tire on a swing that was just swatted by King Kong as my bungee cord whiplashes me in every direction.

Rogerette's face is beet red as she air-swims over and fights to wrangle the squirrel from my mouth. I'm heaving and gasping, my fatigued body yearning to collapse even as my mind is muttering. *If she thinks I'm relinquishing this representation of the ultimate retribution—not to mention my first-ever catching of a squirrel—she's got another think coming because . . .*

"PD, you give me that squirrel this instant!" she yells as she does the Mommy trick of squeezing the sides of my clenched mouth, and within seconds I've released the now slobbery, ripped and torn toy. She gives me a long, icy stare as she pulls the furry plaything close to her eyes, apparently checking whether it's intact enough for another round.

I do a silent *Yessssss!* as she looks at smiley Roger—the latter standing at the head of the treadmill, holding frayed wires and waiting for the verdict—and shakes her head. She throws her hands up in what I recognize as the "PD, I can't take much more! I just can't!" Mommy gesture, then gives an exasperated huff before pointing at researcher Roger to take over the scolding.

He leaves the whiteboard and floats next to me and adopts a softer tone than his colleague. "PD, the goal of this toy reward test was to see if a dog would be motivated to exercise if tempted with a fun toy. We planned to do several runs, each time teasing you with the squirrel in different ways. Since you immediately destroyed the incentive, we can't do more rounds to learn whether a toy can motivate an obese or physically challenged dog to move more and improve its health. See?"

What is he yammering about? I think incredulously. *I got to level 10 in mere seconds solely to get the toy! The toy temptation game clearly works! No need for PD to pass out to prove it!*

Smiley Roger floats over and pats my head. He whispers something about it being okay or something, but I've tuned him and the other Rogers out. My eyes are on a trash bin in the corner of the gym, the lid of which is not totally secure . . .

Because a *tail* is hanging out of it! Apparently Rogerette didn't get the whole toy in there. *I want that squirrel!* I think as I strain against my harness. *Get me off this treadmill! I want my squirrel!*

I whip my head from the trash can back to my teammates as I feel my harness being removed. *Freedom!* I shout to myself as I begin to drift upward. I wiggle around in a happy little dance, knowing that the experiments are over.

And no matter what the Rogers think, I know I aced them all. I (kind of) defeated NutJob! I ate (er, barely tasted) all the alleged foodstuffs! I caught (more than one) Minis! I pursued the (demon in disguise) toy! *I have done Administrator Jetson and all of NASA proud! My work here will lead to groundbreaking, life-changing, trailblazing . . .*

"PD? Please stop banging your paw on the whiteboard!" researcher Roger cries as he grabs one side just before it can topple over. "You look like a preacher pug!"

"He's probably just delirious with hunger," opines egghead Roger as he rubs his own belly. "It's six o'clock and I'm sure we all will be more than happy to leave the gym. I feel like I'm more exhausted than PD gets after yet another flubbed, fumbled failure of an experiment." He notes the nods of agreement, then turns to me. "Well, PD, let's hope NASA has a different definition of success and we don't lose our jobs."

Smiley Roger to the emotional rescue. "Hey! Maybe they do! And it's not like PD didn't try!"

The other Rogers laugh and shake their heads. "I guess," Rogerette says in a kind tone I didn't expect. "We've been hard on you, PD. You *did* pretty much blow all the tests, but . . . we still love you."

I don't know if the emotion overtaking me is due to her unexpected kindness or my fatigue and hunger. But as we all head to the pantry and smiley Roger opens Kibble Bin Three and winks at me as he scoops double my regular amount of food into my bowl, I am thinking of a different bin.

And a few hours later, after watching the Rogers play a few board games and actually getting to enjoy my own Dippin' Dots, I feign sleepiness so that Rogerette will carry me to my sleeping bag before she tucks me in.

After Rogerette heads back to the den to join her colleagues to watch *Alien,* I air-swim lickety-split to the gym trash bin, grab *my* squirrel, and tow it to my bed. Even though we started as enemies, I pretend just for tonight that he is my beloved toy Dog whom I miss so much.

Around midnight, the ship is silent save for smiley Roger's light snoring, which causes me to stir. I am about to gently chew on the toy I am pretending is Dog when in my mind's eye I suddenly am back in the gym and the squirrel again has metamorphosed into that rodent from hell. I take "NutJob" in my teeth and . . .

Chomp!

"PD?" egghead Roger yells as he sneezes. "Why is fur flying everywhere?"

Oops.

Experiment Three
Walkies in zero gravity to reduce obesity
5kg
5kg
NASA
WW
MISSION
TIME: 10:04 LEVEL: 10
SPEED: 9km/hr
STOP
MILK BONE
MILK BONE
NASA
WW
MISSION

NASA

Chapter Seven

WHO LET THE DOG OUT?

In 1972, Brooke Miller of Anaheim, California, invented what is commonly known as the pooper scooper. Her patented two-part system consisted of a long-handled rake and pan, giving dog owners a hands-free, hygienic way to pick up dog waste and deposit it into a bin.

Over the years, Miller's brainchild has seen myriad improvements and alterations, making the chore of poopie pick-up easier as well as more hygienic and eco-friendly: wider scoopers, longer handles, sturdier rakes, springier spring-loaded claws, even sliding levers to lock in odors and LED lights for nighttime use. In the realm of pet care, the pooper scooper truly is considered by many to be among the top innovations.

Unfortunately, this wonderful creation has gone to the dogs. Specifically, *this* dog. Yep, I've gone from first-ever pug in space to first-ever pug on poop patrol. If my Fawn Girl Pug Crush learns of this, she'll never marry me; If Ralph finds out, I'll never live it down.

And it's all because of that stupid fungus food experiment!

I managed to get a pretty good night's rest considering I was roused by egghead Roger for another dressing down after I chewed up my squirrel frenemy and sent faux fur flying all over the sleeping area. But despite yet another lecture my spirits were high, mostly because the dreadful experiments were over. I was looking forward to spending the rest of the mission playing board games and watching movies and getting lots of head pats from smiley Roger.

And getting into Kibble Bin Four and Five.

Alas, it was not to be.

There I was early this morning all snuggy warm in my sleep sack, dreaming that my Fawn Girl Pug Crush was coming down the church aisle toward me, escorted by my groomsdog Rory Rottweiler, while Mommy played Wagner's "Bridal Chorus" on a kazoo. Just as I held my paw out to my bride and the *Vogue Dog* photographer went *snap! snap! snap!*, I was snapped awake by a loud voice tinged with urgency.

"Houston to *Wolf Wanderer*!! Houston to *Wolf Wanderer*!!" a stressed-sounding Administrator Jetson was roaring from the speakers. I peeked out through the opening of my toasty bedroll to see Rogerette hustling out of her own sleeping bag.

"Go ahead, Houston!" she called, the concern in her voice mirroring Administrator Jetson's.

"*Wolf Wanderer* crew," he began, "please remain calm as I tell you that a situation has arisen that must be dealt with posthaste!"

The rest of us hurriedly gathered around Rogerette to learn of a predicament that I feared may have resulted from another boo-boo committed by yours truly.

"At approximately three this morning," the administrator explained, "my overnight team noted a foreign object adhered to an important valve on one of your ship's thermal radiators. As you know, these external panels serve as *Wolf Wanderer*'s cooling system, dispersing the heat generated by the ship's electronics and power systems.

"Superiors were brought in, and within two hours, it was surmised that what they *at first* thought was frozen fecal matter from the waste disposal system was instead . . ."

Suddenly four squinty, squizzy, scowly sets of eyes landed on me . . .

". . . a gooey gob of eel compost."

Oh no, I panicked. *Flee, PD! Air-swim like Katie Ledecky! Hide, PD!*

"After combing through two hours of onboard recordings, the team hypothesized that this gob of eel poop got inside the toilet—how, we are not sure—and during the night was ejected during routine toilet use and ended up stuck to the aforementioned thermal radiator valve and several of the surrounding cooling fins as well."

Eight eyes widened as four heads whipped toward the comm.

"Oh, this is bad!" the normally upbeat smiley Roger gasped. "This means the goo is preventing normal heat dispersal and . . ."

"Exactly!" Administrator Jetson interjected. "Unless it is removed, in mere hours the circuitry that controls *Wolf Wanderer* will overheat, jeopardizing every aspect of functionality including the environmental controls—which, as you might imagine, could have serious consequences."

Geesh! I thought anxiously. *Someone had better fix this and fast! Probably researcher Roger because he's very smart, and . . .*

"PD," the NASA chief said soberly, giving me news I had neither anticipated nor welcomed, "your assistance will be needed on a spacewalk to remove the eel poop glob."

I'm sorry . . . Me? A space walkie? Me?

"While any of your human teammates could do a spacewalk, their hands are too large to access the narrow spaces and surfaces where the eel poop is stuck. So you, PD, will maneuver a very slender titanium probe with a claw on the end to scoop the eel poop off the fins and the valve."

The boss paused and took a very deep breath.

"PD," he said soberly, "as you wield the probe, you must be *very* careful not to pierce any of the fragile tubes alongside the fins! A sloppy slip of a paw could puncture a line! And with the cooling loop compromised, the thermal regulators would not properly dissipate heat generated by your ship's onboard computers, life support and other systems!

"Temperatures would rapidly rise! Systems would fail one by one by one! Soon it would be so hot that neither human nor dog could survive!

"So don't blow it, PD!"

Wolf Wanderer went totally silent as we all took in the enormity of our situation. Plus, I might have passed out for a few minutes, only coming back to consciousness as Administrator Jetson concluded his grim announcement.

"PD, let me be clear: you are the *only* one who can save the ship! Houston out!"

As the NASA boss was signing off, I squeezed my eyes tightly shut, cowered, and put my paws over my ears—because I couldn't bear to see the disappointment in my teammates' eyes. I couldn't bear to hear their rebukes and reproach. I simply was not prepared for the comeuppance that I knew was coming.

That was thirty minutes ago. And as the seconds tick-tick-tick and no screams fill the room, I finally dare to peek around me. Alarmingly, all the Rogers are gone. I am all alone.

I'm feeling very 'fraidy cat, because I now assume that the Rogers all panicked and decided to abandon ship and take their chances in outer space rather than await certain death as I attempt the spacewalk and eel-poop-scooping NASA has tasked me with.

Who would blame them? I mean, they thought they were going to lose their jobs thanks to me. They didn't imagine they'd be losing their *lives* thanks to me.

Just as I turn toward the airlock to see if the Rogers are one-after-the-next bailing out of *Wolf Wanderer*, I hear unexpected giggling behind me.

"Oh it's so cute! Look how tiny it is!" I spin around to see Rogerette holding out what apparently is a mini version of a human spacesuit. Egghead Roger, smiley Roger and researcher Roger are floating in tow, each holding a box. I'm curious about the contents of the parcels, but my eyes are riveted on the little space outfit.

"PD, I have to tell you," Rogerette begins, "we all had to go to the kitchen to confer over the seriousness of this situation and, frankly, to calm our nerves. But we decided that we need to put our faith in you and trust that—despite your having screwed up one task after another—you will succeed in this final assignment and keep us all alive."

"Yeah, little buddy!" smiley Roger sings out.

"You got this, PD!" researcher Roger chimes in.

"Lord help us," egghead Roger groans, adding his typical somber note. He at least softens his verbal smack by adding, "But what choice do we have but to believe there's maybe a ten percent chance we won't burn up this afternoon?"

Researcher Roger is back at his regular spot floating alongside the whiteboard. His body blocks the board as he scribbles away. Over his shoulder he calls, "PD, I know you are never scared when your Mommy takes you on a walkie at home, so there's no need to fear taking a walkie in space, right?"

Um . . .

"You're going on a spacewalk, or what we astronauts call Extra-Vehicular Activity," he explains. "Astronauts go on spacewalks when they need to do maintenance or perform repairs or explore planetary surfaces or . . . remove eel goo stuck on an outer structure that is threatening to end our lives."

I cringe at the words, but he winks as he moves enough for me to see *PD's EVA* underlined at the top of the whiteboard. Underneath, he has written:

Goal: Eel Compost Goo Removal

Site: Thermal Radiator Valve and Adjacent Fins

Steps:

1. PD suits up (check seals, test life support system)

2. PD accompanied into airlock and tethered to ship

3. Airlock opened

4. PD locates goo

5. PD scoops away goo

6. PD returns to ship

I'm staring at the whiteboard as it dawns on me that this is not a fun space movie the Rogers and I are enjoying in the

Wolf Wanderer entertainment room, but rather a space reality show starring me. I'm so entranced that I fail to notice Rogerette and smiley Roger putting what resembles a large diaper on me before they each take a paw and start to put me in my spacesuit. Meanwhile, egghead Roger is pulling items out of boxes; I see gadgets and gizmos I assume are my space equipment.

"PD, give me your hindfoot, please," smiley Roger says as he and Rogerette perform what must be their first-ever attempt to dress a dog in a spacesuit. I am mostly in the suit, but my left hindfoot is sorta bent against the inner layers of spandex and nylon. Smiley Roger quietly grunts as he reaches in and pulls my foot through the opening.

"Aw! You look so cute!" laughs Rogerette as she secures electrodes and a harness to me. "These leads will monitor your vital signs like your heart rate and your respiration.

"And this," she continues as she places a thin cap with ear cups and a mic boom on my wide head, "will attach to your helmet and will allow us to talk to you while you're out there in space!"

Egghead Roger, having finished organizing my spacewalk tools, decides I need another lecture.

"Listen up, PD," he says using his super serious voice. "I know you likely are freaking out. But you can rest assured that your pug spacesuit is designed to keep you alive and well. The inner layers provide life support and cooling; the outer layers provide protection from radiation and extreme temperatures as well as meteoroids and other foreign objects floating around out there.

"So, knowing you are safe, you can concentrate on *keeping all of us alive,* okay?"

You lost me at "meteoroids"! I panic as I scramble my brain for excuses to get out of this. *Surely Rogerette has small enough hands! Surely she can do it! Surely a bit of eel poopie won't make the ship incinerate! I can't do it, I can't do it, I can't do it! I don't want to be meteorized to death! I don't want to be pulverized by gigantic rocks in space!*

"PD! Why are you spinning in circles and barking?" researcher Roger shouts as he grabs onto my right hind paw to halt my twirling and whirling. Unfortunately, being still in body does not translate to being still in mind; I haven't been this anxious since my first bath.

Egghead Roger heads over with what I assume are the contents of those boxes. In one hand is my scooper doodad; it's a long stick thing with teeth on the end. But not scary NutJob teeth; these teeth apparently are for removing the eel poop goo.

Smiley Roger drifts over and holds my paw in what I assume is an attempt to keep me from again bugging out as egghead Roger waves the probe in front of my wide eyes.

"Okay, PD, please pay attention. I'm going to explain your tool kit, the eel goo cleaning procedure, and the tethering system. Then we will get you suited up and I will accompany you into the airlock . . ."

Correction. *Now* my eyes are wide. Like a frog's eyes if you stepped on him. Gigantic, humongous, ginormous squashed frog eyes. I panic as I ponder: *Tool kit? How am I going to hold tools? And cleaning procedure? My specialty is making messes, not cleaning them! Plus I still don't know how to take a walkie in space because there's no air! So I hope my helmet doesn't leak because . . .*

Gradually egghead Roger's voice returns to the fore as I struggle to follow what I'm being told.

". . . and I will tether you to the ship with a pair of retractable lifelines, one primary and one backup. These will be clipped to your spacesuit and then clipped to anchor points in the airlock. That will prevent you from drifting away. Then I will exit the airlock, seal the inner hatch, and finally press the button to open the outer hatch so you can commence your spacewalk and complete your task.

"And just in case something goes wrong and you do become untethered, you'll also be wearing a small, nitrogen-powered jetpack that provides emergency propulsion for untethered astronauts—and dognauts—to return the ship.

"So basically, PD, you couldn't be safer."

Well, actually, yes, I could be safer! I think. *I could be home in Mommy's warm lap instead of leashed to the outside of a spaceship, one mishap away from joining George Clooney drifting out into deep space! Definitely could be safer!*

Rogerette air-sails to me with one hand behind her back and a wide grin on her face that of course makes me wary. But as she shows me what she's hiding, my wariness is replaced with some desperately needed joy.

"PD," she begins as she waves a coveted Dippin' Dots in front of my eyes, "NASA is asking a lot of you—even though it's *entirely* your fault that eel poop goop is stuck to a vital ship component—and I bet you are a bit frightened about your outer space assignment. So we decided you might appreciate a sweet treat before you head out."

Smiley Roger annoyingly tosses in, "Hey, if nothing else, little buddy, think of it as your last supper!"

The gang chuckles at my expense as I accept the flash-frozen beads of yum. *Wow! Cotton Candy flavor!* My whole digestive system does a dance as the ice cream meets my tongue and heads down to my jolly belly. *'Bout time I got a Dippin' Dots! I don't know that I would have volunteered for a space walkie just for this taste sensation, but, well, it's soooo delicious!*

Bringing me back from my gastronomical glee is researcher Roger tapping at his whiteboard. I lick the last few dots from the bottom of the Dippin' Dots pouch and await my instructions.

Researcher Roger points at the board. "Okay, PD, I know you are clear now on when you will get suited up, how your tools work, and how you will be secured to *Wolf Wanderer*. The eel poop scooper will be attached to your right forepaw glove. Once out there, you will be alone but connected to us through your headset. So we will be practically right there with you, okay?"

Not okay, not okay, not okay, not okay, not okay . . .

"Hey! Stop racing around! Get back here!" egghead Roger yells as he tries and fails to grab hold of a paw as I race around the room in a frenzied, frantic attack of the zoomies. "The more you monkey around, the more time ticks by and the greater the chance that this eel compost complication becomes a catastrophe! Now then, it's time to get you in your spacesuit. Remember, this is a life-or-death situation for all of us."

I halt mid-spin as I imagine the goo shutting down the cooling system and my black fur coat catching fire and my sobbing Mommy being handed my charred remains and a melted PD ID tag. Rogerette approaches with my helmet, portable life support backpack, gloves, boots, secondary oxygen pack, and the communication system which she attaches to my soft cap before putting on the rest of my gear except for the helmet, which she explains will come last.

There's no mirror around, but I imagine I must look like a giant marshmallow. But there is no time to think about Mommy and me by the campfire making carob s'mores, because I look up to see egghead Roger floating my way with two long cables, accompanied by smiley Roger who carries a clipboard that holds a checklist on which he is ticking off boxes.

"Okay, we are nearly ready to begin the spacewalk," smiley Roger says, addressing egghead Roger. "You will need to secure PD's helmet, and then we can check his life support pack and make sure his suit is secure. And then you're cleared to head to the airlock."

"Ah-oooooooooo! Ah-oooooooooo! Ah-oooooooooo! Ah-oooooooooo!"

It takes me a beat to realize I'm the reason eight palms have just clamped over four sets of ears. I am howling like our spacecraft's namesake animal.

Researcher Roger again shows his smarts as he snatches my wee helmet from Rogerette and claps it over my wide head, effectively silencing my wailing and whimpering. My final few wails cease, not for lack of fear but because I'm suddenly fascinated by the weird feeling of being inside my helmet. All sounds from the outside are muffled, and I have a panoramic, slightly gold-tinted view of everything. As I look at the Rogers and other objects about me, I feel a bit dizzy and disoriented.

I perceive motion to my left and have to rotate both head and body to slowly swivel myself around. The three Rogers are quietly doing the final checks they discussed earlier while Rogerette, showing a rare mothering love toward yours truly, takes my gloved paw in her hands and stares into my scared wide orbs as my in-helmet audio comes online.

"PD," she says into a microphone, her transmitted voice sounding oddly distant but perfectly clear, "I want you to know that all of us here on *Wolf Wanderer* as well as Administrator Jetson and all of NASA are very proud of our brave little dognaut." Giving my padded forepaw a squeeze I barely sense, she leans closer as she adds, "I know you are scared, but it's time to get out there and get the goo off the ship before your toilet shenanigan causes five deaths!"

As frightened as I am, I find myself following egghead Roger into the *Wolf Wanderer* airlock. I don't think I've ever before dreaded taking a walkie, but here we are. The sole positive about my near-certain demise in space is that I'll be pretty close to Heaven, so God can just reach over and grab my lifeless little body and take me Home.

I need to think of something else. *Something else! Something else! Something else!* And as egghead Roger turns toward me and begins to speak, I realize I am about to have plenty to occupy my terror-filled mind.

"PD, I am tethering you to the anchor points now so you will be very secure as you perform your life-saving task. So there is nothing to fear.

"Ready? Let's go!!"

I give the other Rogers the phony brave expression I wear when getting my annual shots from Dr. Thornton, then follow egghead Roger through the interior hatch and into the airlock chamber that leads to scary outer space. I try not to look at the second hatch, which for me represents the point of no return.

My eyes squeeze shut as egghead Roger places the tethers through loops in my spacesuit and clips them to the anchors positioned near the exterior hatch. I feel him tightening up the straps of my life support pack. And finally, I feel his big hand pat my helmet and hear his final words before he floats over to the interior hatch that he is about to pass back through and then seal.

"Good luck, dognaut PD. We're all counting on you." And with that, he's gone. I never thought I'd miss egghead Roger. But golly, do I ever. As the interior hatch closes, I have never felt more alone, never felt more terrified. I'd give my last bully stick if Sirius would show up and make the eel poop magically disappear.

PD! I admonish my trembling self. *Sirius isn't coming! Pug up! NASA is counting on you!*

I take a deep breath of the recycled pure oxygen provided by my portable life support system, getting a whiff of its faint metallic scent. I hear my rapid inhalations and exhalations and sense the conscious effort needed to make my lungs expand due to my pressurized spacesuit. I feel a slight stream of cool air blowing on my button nose, intended to keep my mask from fogging up.

Enough with the sensory experience tour! Open your eyes! You got this! NASA didn't crown you America's first dognaut for nothing!

The exterior hatch opens, and I paddle out into space.

I fearfully peer around, taking in the blackness, the vastness, the solitariness. I am so alone, all alone. Secluded, separated, sequestered, segregated. *I can't do this. I can't do this. I can't do this . . .*

"Testing! Testing! Testing!" Rogerette's voice booms through my headset, interrupting my pity party. "PD, please check in! PD, please check in! Bark three times to confirm that your communication system is working."

I do the requested woofs and feel calmer knowing that I am connected to the Rogers and not just out here on my lonesome in this ocean of boundless emptiness. But only a bit calmer; I won't be truly anxiety-free until I'm back in the ship snacking on another—well-deserved—Dippin' Dots.

Next I hear the voice of Researcher Roger; apparently he is the one who will oversee Operation Eel Compost Goo Removal. "PD, pay attention, please," he says authoritatively yet calmly. "I want you to find the thermal valve on the flat radiator panel. Go to your left and walk through space toward it. Bark when you see the cooling fins with the goo stuck to them."

I take a final moment to center myself and appreciate the majesty of the starlit heavens. I imagine Sirius the Dog Star looking at PD the mini Dog Star with what I hope is admiration but fear is trepidation since he knows I'm light-years out of my league on this task. But here goes . . .

I push myself off the ship's surface, then bound through space toward the offending eel poo goo. When my fear mounts, I distract myself by momentarily shutting my eyes and imagining Mommy at a big NASA ceremony where Administrator Jetson is attaching a *Dognaut Medal of Heroism* pin to my collar as my Fawn Girl Pug Crush weeps with pride from the front row and Ralph the Dog is blasted away to Neptune and . . .

"PD? PD? PD!!!" Researcher Roger's alarmed voice snaps me out of my daydream, and I am terrified to see *Wolf Wanderer* is suddenly far off in the distance—eighty-five feet in the distance, to be exact. I know this factoid because Mommy read that that's the full length of the tethers that connect astronauts to the spaceship on EVAs. And believe you me, my tethers are fully tethering! The cables are all the way extended and taut, and I am twisting and twirling and swiveling and swirling in space as I try and fail to grab the lines and pull myself in.

And I thought my helmet was fogged up before. And I thought my heart was at maximum at level 10 on the treadmill. And I thought NutJob was the scariest thing I'd ever encounter. And I thought . . .

"PD! It's okay, little buddy," says smiley Roger, who clearly has been chosen as the Roger to talk me off the proverbial ledge. "You just took a bit a farther-out walkie than intended, but don't you fret—we are going to guide you back, okay?"

I slow my breathing and follow his cues, straddling the tether lines and inchworming my way back toward the goo that by now has had another half hour to cause our incineration.

"Okay, listen up," researcher Roger begins after I am at my destination. He calls my attention to the thingy attached to my glove—"the miniature titanium probe," as he calls it—and tells me to use it and its clawed end to scoop and scrape the eel poo off the radiator's delicate components. I feel like a neurosurgeon employing exacting precision as I begin, remembering that any mistake could . . .

"PD!" yells a suddenly panicked researcher Roger, choosing the worst time to blare into my helmet. "You must be *very* careful not to pierce any of the fragile coolant tubes alongside the fins! One slipshod slip of a paw could spell our doom! If the cooling loop gets compromised, the thermal regulators will not properly dissipate heat generated by *Wolf Wanderer*'s onboard computers, life support and other systems!

"Death for us all, PD! Death!"

Not helpful, researcher Roger! I grumble inwardly as my little paws in my little gloves guide the titanium probe back and forth, over and over. I marvel that that slender, lightweight space stick is rigid enough to dislodge the thick goo without bending, and that the barbed, clawed other end can hook into the goo without scratching the delicate radiator fins.

I am painstakingly careful and exact as I scrape a tiny bit of the goo off and repeat the process over and over. I feel about as delicate as that fat hippo in the tutu in *Fantasia* as I work to not stumble, bumble or fumble this operation all up. But there is so much goo! *So many teeny tiny fins! So much! So many! So much! So many!*

"Hey, PD! It's looking good on our cameras!" sounds Rogerette's voice in my helmet. "Administrator Jetson called in to say the overheating system alarm is diminishing in volume! Keep at it!"

An hour or so later, my tired forepaw is still *scrape, scrape, scraping* to clear up the tiny bits of eel compost stubbornly sticking to the thermal fins. I am so weary. I would give anything—even that coveted Dippin' Dots—to be home in my bed, or even in my *Wolf Wanderer* sleep sack. But I have come so far. *I can finish! Just another three or four bits of goo to go; if I can just get in there, just work the probe in and . . .*

Decimation! Destruction! Obliteration! Annihilation! Extinction!

The explosion around me is both blindingly bright and eerily silent. My sole positive thought is that with my vision gone, I don't have to witness the bodies of the Rogers drifting into the great void; I don't have to see the deaths I caused. And as the light grows yet brighter, as my retinas sense flash after flash, as I imagine the ship blowing up over and over . . . I float Home to God and Sirius, hoping Mommy will know I tried. *I really tried, Mommy. I really, really tried.*

* * *

"Hey! His hind paw just twitched!"

The sound of smiley Roger's cheery voice cuts through the blackness of my muddled mind and rouses me to consciousness. I slowly open my eyes, expecting to see him and the other Rogers clad in radiant white linen garments adorned with gold sashes and halos, beautiful harps at their feet.

But . . .

Oh no! I think, peering around me. *I thought I was Good Dog during my life. But the Rogers aren't in angel suits! Was I Bad Dog? Is this Bad Dog Place?*

"Welcome back, little buddy," says smiley Roger as he takes my shaky forepaw in his warm hand. "You've had quite the adventure, haven't you?"

The other Rogers gather 'round, all grinning widely.

Disorientation and confusion threaten to overwhelm me as I look around the *Wolf Wanderer* entertainment room, where I'm tethered to a comfy couch. I will my brain to make sense of the scene. The last thing I remember is being on my scary space walkie, attempting to clear the sticky eel stuff from the radiator and save everyone from burning up, and then doing a final scrape and then an explosion of light!

And then Sirius taking my paw as we floated away, away, away . . .

"PD, you saved us all!" Rogerette sings out. "But just as you were finishing your task, you apparently experienced what's called a cosmic ray visual phenomenon."

Huh? No! There was a big bright boom! And then I went bye-bye!

Egghead Roger chimes in. "See, PD, what happened is that some high-energy space particles passed directly through your retinas, causing your brain to perceive flashes of light that weren't actually there."

Researcher Roger leans in, taking in my bewildered expression. "PD, cosmic ray visual phenomena are common and harmless. You hyperventilated and fainted. But all's good, PD, all's good.

"In fact, all is *great*. You completed your mission, PD. You saved our lives."

Just as my baffled brain is registering that I did not die but merely passed out and that I'm safe and sound back on the spaceship with the Rogers, a loud squawk draws our attention to the comm.

"Houston to *Wolf Wanderer*, Houston to *Wolf Wanderer* . . ."

A very happy smiley Roger replies, "Go ahead, Houston! We have a revived superhero dognaut standing by with us!"

Egghead Roger removes the safety straps so I can float freely. I stretch my furry body and stand tall as I excitedly await the sound of our boss' voice.

The speaker crackles to life, and I hear a deep breath.

"PD, in the long history of NASA, I don't think we have ever experienced so much sheer terror and sheer exhilaration on the same day," Administrator Jetson says, his emotion evident as he speaks. "When my crack team was alerted to the presence of the life-threatening eel compost muck stuck to the *Wolf Wanderer* cooling fins, and when they then ascertained that only *you*, PD, could save the crew, well, I have to admit there was a moment when I figured you all were goners."

Under his breath, egghead Roger grumbles, "Yeah, especially since he caused the goo to be stuck to the fins in the first place!"

The big boss pauses, and I hear what sounds like an object being set on a desk. "Thank you, Deputy," he says to someone near him before returning to the mic. "PD, NASA will be mounting a plaque in our conference room recognizing your fearlessness, your courageousness, your dauntlessness out in space today. You forever will be remembered as the dognaut who saved *Wolf Wanderer* and its crew from incineration.

"I salute you, PD. NASA salutes you. Houston out!"

My pounding happy heartbeat reverberates in my ears as the administrator signs off and silence fills the ship. I glance around me to see the Rogers exhibiting something I haven't noticed aimed my way since we boarded the ship days ago.

Pride.

Of course, egghead Roger can't resist reminding me why the space walkie was necessary in the first place.

"Nice work, PD. But if I find anything—and I do mean *anything*—in my bed tonight that shouldn't be there, I will toss you right outside into space with nothing but your mechanical squirrel buddy to keep you company. Got it?"

The mention of NutJob nearly sends me spiraling from happiness to horror. But as a grinning Rogerette air-swims over and reveals what she has hidden behind her back, my joy returns tenfold.

A banana split Dippin' Dots!

Best day ever.

NASA
HERO

Wolf Wanderer

EPILOGUE

"PD, honey, it's almost time. Let me straighten your wolf pin." Mommy is fussing over me for what must be the tenth time since we arrived at the NASA auditorium for this ceremony celebrating the *Wolf Wanderer* mission.

I'm sitting tall in my padded chair at our table nearest the stage; I might be back on Earth, but I'm feeling over the moon with pride, my barrel chest puffed out to near-bursting.

And I look so very dapper in the dressy black satin harness Mommy bought me to match her black satin dress. And I have clean smell from bath time and clipped nails and a wiped nasal fold and everything. If only my Fawn Girl Pug Crush could see how dandified and debonair I am.

Tonight's event comes a week after *Wolf Wanderer* landed in Florida following what the news media nicknamed "Spectacle in Space." Somehow, thankfully, reporters didn't mention how the eel poopie found its way onto the hull; they simply focused on how America's first dognaut, PD the Pug, succeeded in removing the stuck muck and saving both the ship and its crew.

My treatment on the trip back to terra firma was markedly different from when I was getting stink-eyed right and left for botched experiments and "creative" concealments of foodstuffs and freaked-out zoomies and just lots of shenanigans, tomfoolery and basically making a mess of things. I seemingly went from worst to first in the Rogers' eyes. Even egghead Roger was, well, less mean to me, going as far as to let me have the last of his Dippin' Dots when he saw me drooling as he about to spoon the frozen beads of yum into his mouth.

Now as I await the start of the reception, I glance around the crowded room until I spot the Rogers. They all look as delighted to be here as I am. And why wouldn't they? I mean, just over a week ago they thought they were facing the unemployment line; now they're likely in line for promotions and pay raises.

I catch the sparkling eye of smiley Roger at the table to our right just as he whispers something to an equally happy-looking woman I assume is Mrs. Smiley Roger. He winks at me and gives me his customary thumbs up, causing me to do a little wiggle in my seat as I recall his many—usually undeserved—cheer-fueled words of encouragement during our mission.

I'm about to wave my paw in response when a bright spotlight hits the podium on the stage. It's a good thing Mommy took me to see a "veterinary behavioralist" because for several days after I got home I was having full-blown panic attacks whenever she turned on a light and I relived the ship's explosion, er, the "cosmic ray visual phenomenon" thingy. The money she shelled out was well worth it, because the spotlight on the podium doesn't cause me to howl in horror.

Mommy gives my head a loving pat as Frank Sinatra's "Come Fly with Me" plays in the auditorium. I spot researcher Roger, seated a couple of tables away, tapping his fingers to the beat. At the table next to his, egghead Roger is sitting alongside Rogerette, both of them looking absolutely tickled to be here. Yep, egghead Roger, tickled pink! Who'da thought?

I squirm in my chair as the music fades and the audience falls silent in what feels like electrified anticipation. This room is filled with current and former astronauts, top NASA officials, congressional leaders who deal with space policy, that SpaceX guy, and lots of other nibs, nobs, notables and nabobs—all of them looking as chuffed to be here as I am.

"Ladies and gentlemen!" A deep baritone voice commands the attention of the room. "Please give a warm welcome to NASA's 'out of this world' leader . . . Administrator George Jetson!"

The crowd hurrays and hurrahs as I watch our boss stride on stage, position himself behind the podium, and adjust the mic. I close my eyes and imagine myself back on *Wolf Wanderer*, recalling him telling me the importance of each experiment I was about to embark on: the squirrel chase, the faux food tastings, the treadmill test, and finally the EVA. All the tests and trials that led to my being here tonight.

"Enough, enough!" the administrator playfully admonishes the loudly cheering gathering, most of whom are on their feet. "Thanks so much for your warm welcome, but please be seated."

He waits for everyone to settle back in their seats—and for me to stop spinning in circles—and then consults his small stack of note cards.

"In the history of this fine organization I am honored to lead, NASA has awarded the prestigious Space Medal of Honor to just twenty-eight astronauts."

His eyes roam the large room before landing on me. His smile actually might be smilier than smiley Roger's as he continues.

"But tonight, we bestow our twenty-ninth Space Medal of Honor on not only the newest member of our NASA family but also—and I know I speak for everyone here tonight—the bravest . . ."

I glance two tables over and note egghead Roger's exasperated eye roll.

". . . as well as perhaps the top contributor—thanks to his successful work during all of his onboard trials—to important NASA research and the development of life-*enhancing*, life-*bettering*, life-*extending* technologies."

And now it's research Roger's turn to smack his head in disbelief.

The boss continues: "Let me tell you all about PD the Pug, America's first dognaut, the star of what our media friends have dubbed 'Spectacle in Space.' The pug who removed the life-threatening eel compost that somehow found its way into the thermal cooling fins on the exterior of the ship . . ."

Here Rogerette grinds her teeth with such force that I'm certain the entire audience hears it.

". . . risking his own life to save the lives of his crewmates."

I force myself to not peek at smiley Roger, too afraid I won't see his signature thumbs-up. I couldn't bear it.

Administrator Jetson pauses and appears to wipe his eyes. "Saving five lives and the *Wolf Wanderer* spacecraft might be this brave dognaut's most important feat, but it's far from his only feat. Let me tell you what his outstanding, exceptional, brilliant work on this mission will mean for both humans and canines now and into the future.

"In addition to the famous deed you've all learned about through extensive media coverage, our PD the dognaut will forever be remembered for his contribution to scientific innovations and advancements. These amazing developments are the direct result of his participation in the *Wolf Wanderer* mission's three crucial experiments. Indeed, PD's amazing success in the space trials was far beyond what NASA could have hoped for or imagined when he was selected from the tens of thousands of dogs that applied for the dognaut position and . . ."

The "Harrumph!" from egghead Roger is so loud that Administrator Jetson appears to momentarily lose his place in his speech. He looks around the room for the source of the interruption before shuffling through his note cards and resuming.

"The first trial, *Pug Rodent Pursuit in Zero Gravity: Implications for Advancements in Olympic and Other Athletic Training,* saw how a pug chasing a mechanical squirrel in a frantic, frenzied, fast and furious challenge could lead to revolutionary products for America's Olympians as well as athletes at every level from Peewee, Pop Warner, and T-ball to collegiate and professional sports."

The room momentarily spins as I recall the *click-click-clicking* of NutJob's metal nails and the *clack-clack-clacking* of his sharp teeth. I feel moments from passing out as I relive being tossed into Kibble Bin One over and over. Mommy must notice my shaking limbs, because I feel her fingers loop around my harness to both calm me and restrain any zoomie that might try and possess me.

The administrator waves at a table full of lean but fit-looking men and women, all of whom are wearing gold medals on blue ribbons around their necks.

"Our nation's track and field Olympians—like the esteemed gold medalists who've honored us with their presence here tonight—only reach this championship level through intense training that requires focus, reaction time and stamina. And now, thanks to PD's *own* focus, reaction time and stamina during his squirrel chase, there is about to be a revolutionary change in athletic training.

"In essence, researchers studying PD's movement patterns and intestinal fortitude while in pursuit of the rodent determined that if this effort could be recreated in the athletic training world, our athletes potentially could gain a huge competitive edge."

Administrator Jetson pauses to look my way.

"So, thanks to our dognaut PD, I am excited to announce that athletes looking to qualify for the Olympics will soon have the option to train with 'PD the Pug's Robotic Training Companion.' These life-sized 'squirrel-bots' are designed to push athletes' physical and mental limits, leading to a new form of endurance training where athletes must track and chase a constantly moving target across varied terrains.

"PD, on behalf of America's Olympians, thank you for helping them to bring home more gold medals than ever before!"

The room explodes in roaring applause. Even that famous SpaceX man is on his feet. Researcher Roger is grinning as he offers me what I hope isn't a mock salute; both smiley Roger and Mrs. Smiley Roger give me a thumbs up. I spy Rogerette nudging egghead Roger to join the standing ovation; he slowly rises but looks decidedly less enthusiastic than the guests around him.

Administrator Jetson lifts a hand and waits for the assemblage to sit back down before consulting his notes.

"But while improved training for America's top athletes is noteworthy," he says, beaming at me, "PD's achievements in the other two experiments actually are far more remarkable, extraordinary, incredible and *significant.* Because his successes in these other two trials are going to improve the health and *lives* of both humans and canines."

He pauses here to take in the room, I guess giving his audience a moment to take in the magnitude of what yours truly has accomplished. I'm already on cloud nine over having a robot trainer named after me; I sure didn't expect to learn that any of my experiments, er, "successes" will save lives.

I glance over and see that, seemingly as one, researcher Roger, Rogerette and egghead Roger—sadly, even smiley Roger—have buried their faces in their hands, shaking their heads in disbelief and exasperation. To her credit, Rogerette at least offers me a small grin when she looks up and notices I'm looking her way.

"PD's second test was of particular importance to NASA," the administrator says as he acknowledges a table of men and women clad in blue suits and dresses, each adorned with NASA's coveted *Silver Snoopy* pin given to non-astronauts who've made special contributions to missions. "Because this experiment, *Pug Olfactory Influence on Ingestion Choices: Implications for Astronaut Palate Fatigue and Sustenance Sustainability on Future Multi-Year Missions,* is going to lead to healthier astronauts during space endeavors and also"—here he pats his protruding gut and guffaws—"much happier mealtimes while in space!

"This crucial test saw our dognaut using his unique pug sense of smell to bravely sample unfamiliar futuristic foodstuffs. And he set aside his own food preferences as he ate *every* bite of the samplings."

The snort from researcher Roger causes me to look around for a horse that may somehow have trotted into the auditorium.

"PD," the boss continues, "as we told you when you embarked on this second trial, our astronauts too often come home from missions exhibiting loss of muscle and bone mass due in part to unappealing and/or repetitive meals. Since your canine olfactory system is up to a hundred thousand times more sensitive than a human's, your amazing sense of smell helped you rate foods on their spiciness, aromas and other traits that will stimulate astronauts' dulled palates and encourage them to eat more and stay strong and healthy during missions."

He takes in the Rogers and the NASA officials. "Additionally, as NASA flight crews of the future voyage out of Earth's orbit to Mars and even beyond, they must have nutritious foods that can be stored long-term and also be assembled as needed, like with the 3-D-printed pizza PD enjoyed.

"Yes, thanks to PD, astronauts will have access to new foods like succulent synthetic steaks; delicious repurposed fungus; scrumptious gourmet insects; and"—I note Administrator Jetson has gone a tad green as he takes a deep breath—"well, um, other delectable additions to mission menus that I have been assured are going to have our astronauts coming back for seconds and thirds at mealtime.

"And I'm thrilled to announce tonight that the containers of all these new foodstuffs will bear the label *PD Provisions* and feature the image of our dognaut PD wearing his *Wolf Wanderer* pin so that the astronauts of today and tomorrow will remember PD the Pug's role in their tastier meals and their healthier bodies."

Mommy strokes my paw as the audience again rises and cheers. I give my widest snagglesmile and do my waggiest tail wag. I'm happy to note that all the Rogers are clapping enthusiastically; I want it to be out of love for me, but I suspect it's at least partly because, as astronauts, this experiment is going to impact their and their colleagues' health.

"The final test," the NASA boss goes on as the applause dies down, "might be *PD's* favorite." His eyes twinkle as he looks my way.

"I'm sure many of us here tonight have some of the aches and pains that come with being aging, obesity and even genetics. But imagine being an obese, physically challenged or lame canine who desperately needs to exercise but cannot easily do so . . . leading to continued weight gain and worsening joint disease, hip dysplasia, and other mobility issues.

"Well, thanks to PD, those dogs most in need of movement who cannot *do* that movement without increased pain and discomfort soon will be enjoying pain-free walks. And this hopefully will bring about not only a decrease in achiness and stiffness but also a marked reduction in weight."

Another wink my way. "Who knew a pug could take on Usain Bolt?" Administrator Jetson accepts polite laughter from the audience.

"This study, titled *Pug Walks in Zero Gravity: Impacts on Canine Exercise Motivation and Reduction of Canine Obesity and Associated Poor Health,* had our PD walking and running on a special treadmill. The dozens of air nozzles in this futuristic machine's belt enabled PD—outfitted in a securely tethered harness—to alternate between walking on the belt and levitating just above it. Over and over and over."

I hear the Rogers chortle over the use of the word *walking.* I recall the anxiety I went through as so-called "walking" became level 10 galloping as that mechanical arm walloped me with Milk-Bone Minis.

"And again, all because of PD the Pug, obese, diseased and physically challenged dogs will enjoy walks that mimic walking in zero gravity," the administrator says excitedly. "Yes! Imagine your arthritic or obese or otherwise challenged fur baby alongside you, happily roaming the block, sniffing the sniffs and smelling the smells as your remote control enables the pooch to alternate between walking on the ground and hovering an inch or so above it—bounding as lightly as astronaut Genc Cernan did in the reduced gravity of the moon—as they burn off calories without damaging their joints.

"It will soon be possible, thanks to the PD Hover Harness." Holding up a black dog harness, a dog-sized parachute pack, and a remote control, he continues, "This incredible piece of technology will change the lives of dogs heretofore unable to comfortably exercise. The human-controlled remote will let dogs walk in near-weightlessness." Turning to me again, he says, "I can't exactly speak for our canine friends, but I know they join me in barking out their thanks for what I know is a coming reduction in obesity and resultant joint pain and chronic health conditions in overweight and senior dogs."

He again wipes his eyes, and I have to wonder if he has a physically challenged furry friend waiting for him at home.

"PD, on behalf of NASA, let me again thank you. Your outstanding work on *Wolf Wanderer* seems, well, otherworldly—almost as if you had supernatural assistance as you aced test after test."

And then he shocks me by what he says as he looks heavenward.

"PD, did you know that there is an actual Dog Star out in space named Sirius? It's the biggest star in our galaxy! I bet Sirius is so very, very proud of you for all you've done for mankind and dogkind, PD. I'll bet Sirius considers you Earth's very own Dog Star. We at NASA sure do.

"Ladies and gentlemen, let's give one more shout out to PD the PugNaut, America's awesome—pawsome—pug!"

And as thunderous applause fills the auditorium—the four Rogers actually cheering the loudest—I raise my proud face toward the ceiling, offering a heartfelt thanks to my friend Sirius for guiding me through those "successful" experiments.

And just when I think things couldn't get any better . . .

"Psst. PD, I've got something for you," smiley Roger stage-whispers from his nearby table as he reaches into his pocket and holds out a . . . Dippin' Dots!

* * *

The flight home to Arlington, Virginia, from Florida sure seemed slow. And being in my crate by Mommy's feet in our business-class seat was a not as fun as floating around the spaceship. And the lack of a media circus at baggage claim brought my ego firmly back down to Earth, for sure.

But this afternoon, as I snuggle up to Mommy in the aptly named cuddle chair, there's nowhere I'd rather be than home sweet home. Because, as Mommy reminds me as she fingers the *Wolf Wanderer* collar I hope she never takes off me so that Ralph will see it every time I encounter his sorry self on walkies . . .

"You might be NASA's new Dog Star, PD, but to me, you shined as brightly before the launch as you do today. You're still the same twinkling, dazzling, radiating PD who lights up my heart, *Wolf Wanderer* mission or not."

Well, okay, but let me know when we are going to the National Air and Space Museum, because I'm very excited to see the new PD the PugNaut Spacesuit exhibit. . . .

GET IN TOUCH WITH PD!

You can write to him at

PD the Pug Productions
2200 Wilson Boulevard
Suite 102-265
Arlington, VA 22201

Or give him a shout at

pdthepug@gmail.com

ABOUT PD

In 2021, when he wrote his premier masterpiece, *Get Me Out of Here! Reflections of PD the Put-Upon Pug*, PD could not have envisioned he soon was to become the dog darling of the literary world.

He has been featured in *Modern Dog* and *Dogster* magazines as well as having his books named twice on their top products pages. He has been interviewed twice on the internationally known Australia-based *Pug Life Show* podcast as well as on several radio broadcasts and has been highlighted in national dog blogs. He has participated in more than 50 book signings at major dog fests and other top dog events as well as in dozens of dog retail stores.

Beyond accolades for his waggishly witty, un-put-downable writings, PD is well known in the canine world for dozens of stunningly noteworthy achievements, including:

- Fastest Zoomies at Bath Time Award as clocked by the National Race Car Association
- Longest Wizzie Award as measured by the Institute for Canine Flow Dynamics

- Neighborhood Watchdog Golden Gaze Award for most hours spent staring out the window at nothing, presented by the National Canine Vigilance Association
- Fastest Consumption of Kibble at Dinnertime as timed by the Royal Order of the Hoover Hounds

At press time, PD was sitting by Mommy's phone, waiting to hear from the nominating committee of the Puglitzer Prize Board at Cambridge Canine University.

Space Cadet! PD the Pug and the Final Frontier is PD's sixth book.

ABOUT MOMMY

Mommy Marilee Joyce thanks her luckiest stars every day that her little space cadet PD is part of her life.

From the day she brought him home from Howling Hills Kennel, she has had the privilege of feeding, walking, bathing and grooming him; getting the goopies out of his googly eyes; picking up his whoopsies; and explaining that it is merely his reflection he is barking at in the sliding glass door and not a threat to Mommy, his toys or his treats.

When Mommy is not cuddling and snuggling PD, she is running Joyce Communications in Washington, DC, and PD the Pug Productions. She has served as an anchor and reporter for several television affiliates. In Washington, she has produced and hosted television programs from Capitol Hill, and her company currently offers full video and audio production services.

Mommy is amazed daily that she lives with such a genius dog. She spied him the other day knocking his flat face against the computer keyboard, working on book seven. . . .

OTHER BOOKS BY PD THE PUG

Get Me Out of Here! Reflections of PD the Put-Upon Pug

No, YOU Sit! PD the Pug's Manual for How to Train Your Human

Working Like A . . . Dog! PD the Pug in Corporate America

A Star Is Born! PD the Pug on the Silver Screen

Furry Fairy Tales: PD the Pug's Bedtime Stories

www.ingramcontent.com/pod-product-compliance
Lightning Source LLC
Chambersburg PA
CBHW071307030726
47594CB00002B/343

* 9 7 8 1 9 7 2 4 4 6 0 9 6 *